MORE TALES OF THE
OLD POACHERS

MORE TALES OF THE
OLD
POACHERS

JOHN HUMPHREYS

Illustrations by
JOHN PALEY

David & Charles

BY THE SAME AUTHOR

Living Off the Land
Hides Calls and Decoys
The Sportsman Head to Toe
Modern Pigeon Shooting
Stanley Duncan, Wildfowler
The Shooting Handbook (Ed)
The Do-It-Yourself Gameshoot
Learning to Shoot
The Woods Belong to Me (Ed)
Hunter's Fen
Shooting Pigeons
The Country Sportsman's Record Book & Journal
The Complete Gundog
Poachers' Tales
Days and Nights on Hunter's Fen
The Complete Rough Shoot
The Complete Game Shoot

Illustrations by John Paley

A DAVID & CHARLES BOOK

Text copyright © John Humphreys 1995
First published 1995
Reprinted 1996

A catalogue record for this book is available from the British Library.

ISBN 0 7153 0185 3

Typeset by ABM Typographics Limited, Hull
and printed in Great Britain by
Bath Press Colourbooks
for David & Charles
Brunel House   Newton Abbot   Devon

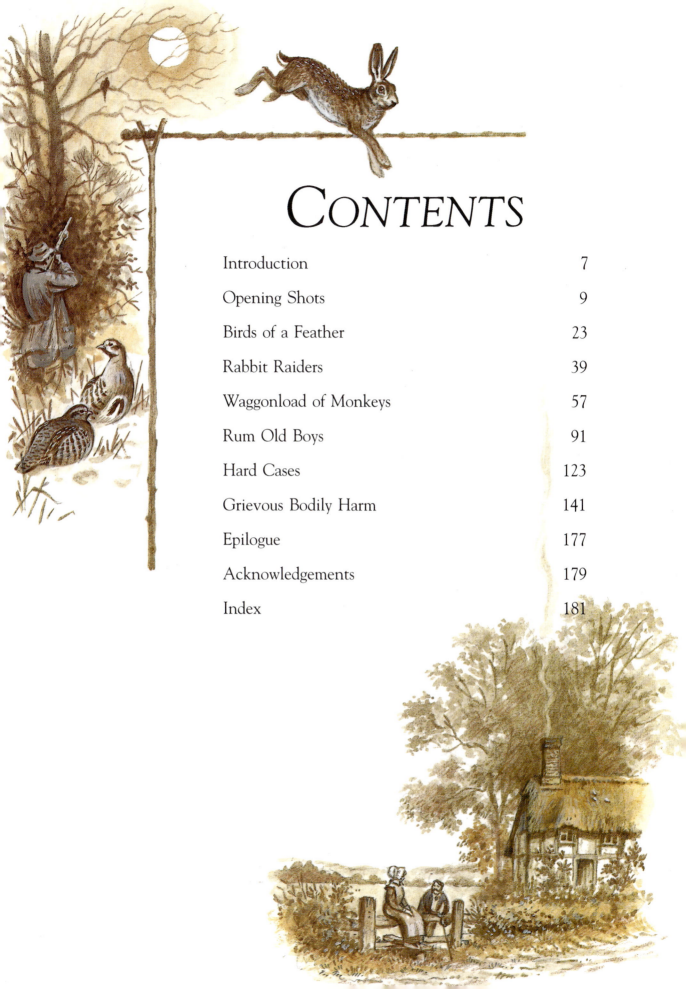

CONTENTS

INTRODUCTION

My book *Poachers' Tales* (David & Charles, 1991) provoked a surprising amount of interest. The cocktail of lawlessness, the countryside and times past seemed hard to resist, for it touched on an ancient nerve buried deep in us all. Stealing a pheasant from a rich man who owned thousands of them has a basic appeal; doing it at risk of a thrashing from keepers and the horror of the law courts in order to feed a hungry family gives the act provenance: what would we not give to have the courage to do such a thing ourselves? It was inevitable that the moment the book was in print new stories should come flooding in, and this sequel is a further collection of poaching yarns.

Some of the characters who have crawled out of the woods and onto the pages are fascinating, all of them now returned to the dust whence they sprang, and it is unlikely in this urbanised age of computer technology that we shall see their like again. 'Rabbity' Dick, Old 'Lijah, the Fox Twins, Donald the deer poacher and Kenzie Thorpe are some of them, curious anachronisms born out of their time and who, had they lived two centuries ago, would have been executed or deported for piracy or highway robbery.

Some of the characters are especially unsavoury such as murderous 'Sloppy' Hammerton, and the Sergeant of Dragoons who had his arm chopped off in a fight with keepers, and possibly worst of all, MacCurrochie of Sutherland, who would shoot an arrow at a passing stranger just for sport. There was the fearful Blucher, the boar hound/mastiff cross which all but killed a gamekeeper, man traps, cruel magistrates, desperate affrays and cruel death in the moonlit corridors of the silent woodlands. The yarns lose nothing in the telling – but it is curious, if not surprising, that those told by keepers reflect the stupidity of poachers, while the poachers have the opposite tale to tell.

The modern poacher tends to be a bully and a thief, quite prepared to attack and even murder a keeper or fire a farmer's ricks; his knowledge of the countryside is scant, and by brute force and ignorance he steals another man's work, not to eat the pheasants himself but to sell them, and only for a paltry sum, what is more, because the game market is depressed these days. The old poacher was an artist and a country craftsman, and even the keeper gave him grudging respect.

No one has the need to poach any more, whereas once it was a way of life and many a family kept hunger at bay by taking rabbits when and where they could. The risks were fearful, and under the original Game Laws a man could be mangled in a man-trap (the 'Iron Wolf'), shot with a spring gun or deported for bagging one of the many animals or birds which positively swarmed in the countryside around – and he with hungry children at home. The law by which the birds of the air and hares of the field, with the freedom to cross boundaries at will, could be said to be 'owned' by anyone was a difficult one with which to come to terms.

Here is a further collection of stories from the hard old days, and I am grateful to the ex-poachers and old keepers who have sent me their reminiscences. I am grateful also to those publishers and authors who have given permission for their stories to be reproduced here. Every effort has been made to contact those whose work is included in the pages which follow.

INTRODUCTION

My own career as a poacher was short, inglorious and culminated in the early 1960s in Oakham Magistrates Court with a fine of £13 for shooting a pheasant, which belonged to someone else, with a .22 rifle. I could not even claim that I was carrying out that dastardly act in an attempt to seek authentic first-hand copy for *Poachers' Tales* because the book lay thirty years in the future. I simply wanted a good dinner which, to an impoverished student, was a rare enough event. However, for a short moment I shared an experience with Kenzie Thorpe, the Fox Twins and other rascals who never seemed to learn from their mistakes – as I did. Unlike them, I was not 'a natural'.

Now, I prefer to curl up o'nights and pull the blankets over my head in that perfect poaching weather when the wind roars and the moon sails past on a sea of choppy clouds. As for brawling with keepers thirty a-side with clubs and dog spears under the great oak as did the ill-fated Sergeant of Dragoons, I am more than happy to leave that to those with the stomach for it.

Flashes the blood-red gleam
Over the midnight slaughter;
Wild shadows haunt the stream;
Dark forms glance o'er the water.
It is the leisterers' cry!
A salmon, Ho! O ho!
In scales of light, the creature bright
Is glimmering below.

Anon – nineteenth-century

OPENING SHOTS

The following delightful statement by an anonymous Warwickshire poacher long since gathered to his fathers says much of what this book is about. His philosophy is one with which even the most ardent squire, keeper or game preserver must feel a sneaking sympathy:

'I once nearly set a rick afire by firing my gun in the stackyard at some partridges, the wad falling into the hay, but for God's mercy there was no wind that night and I beat out the sparks with my hat. The safest time to poach is of a Sunday morning in the forenoon when other law abiding folks be at their praying, meals and afterwards to their rest. The fields are deserted then and no farmer will be astir until three of the clock.

'I never sold any of the birds I shot, nor any of the rabbits or hares. I poached solely for my own savoury pot and for my wife and baby girl. We never wanted for good meat and we devoured what I shot with much relish, more perhaps than if we had come by the meat in a legitimate way. For there were awful risks attached to this lust of mine, for lust it was, not only because we were a' hungry and poor but also because I was never so happy as when I had a gun in my hands.

'I dare to swear that the grand squire and his spoilt rich friends did not enjoy their sumptuous dinners half as much as Meg, Jenny and I. Little labour and no skill had gone to the shooting of their game whilst on my side there was hunger to spur me on and poverty and the knowledge, all the time, that were I caught by the squire or the keepers that would be the end of my job as cowman at the manor farm, and my livelihood. We should have been banished to another country where we would have no friends and relatives and possibly no roof to shelter us from the Winter skies.

'I never stole fruit or livestock, ducks, hens or sheep, but the wild things of the woods and fields I stole, if you can call shooting a rich man's game by so harsh a word.'

Anon – nineteenth-century poacher

· JOHN GAY ON JUSTICE ·

The poet Gay takes a satirical look at the magistrates who enforced with such zeal the Game Laws which they had put in place to protect their own sport:

A Justice with grave Justices shall sit,
He praise their wisdom, they admire his wit.
No greyhound shall attend the tenant's pace,
No rusty gun the farmer's chimney grace;
Salmons shall leave their covers void of fear,
Nor dread the thievish net or triple spear;
Poachers shall tremble at his awful name,
Whom vengeance now o'ertakes for murdered game.

John Gay (1685–1732)

· 'STONEHENGE' ON POACHING ·

In 1856, the author and countryman 'Stonehenge' wrote a massive and comprehensive work entitled British Rural Sports *(Routledge & Co) which included, among others, angling, equestrianism, skating, sailing, shooting and greyhound racing. The tome ran to many hundreds of pages printed in minuscule typeface which even with modern lighting is difficult to read. I wonder if anyone has ever read it from cover to cover. He had advice for keepers troubled with poachers, guidance based, one suspects, on hearsay, wishful thinking, a modest understanding of the subject and a naive acceptance that the 'gentleman poacher' was by no means as reprehensible as the 'poaching labourer'. 'Stonehenge' was more at home with greyhounds than mouchers.*

His advice to keepers to 'keep the menace at bay' shows a touching and probably ill-founded trust in the willingness of the farm labourer to inform on his mates in return for an extra five bob in his pay packet at Christmas, with or without the moral support of a 'railway whistle' for the more unwelcome visitors from London. However, 'Stonehenge' spoke of the age in which he lived when poaching was seen as a serious rural menace, especially by the squirearchy for whom he wrote, and at a time when the penalties for transgression were almost medieval.

'With regard to the poacher, everything depends on the labourers on the farms. If they like to countenance the poacher or if they are unfortunately poachers themselves, all the efforts of the keeper will be of little avail. The best plan is to make all the labourers feel an interest in the preservation of the game. Let every man receive at Christmas a certain sum proportionate to the head of game killed during the season and the outlay will be found to be well bestowed, since it will go much further than the same sum laid out an extra watchers. I have known 650 acres of land preserved entirely in the neighbourhood of a large town without any regular keeper and with an outlay in the shape of presents to labourers certainly not exceeding £20 per year.

'On this farm hares were as thick as sheep and partridges sufficient to allow thirty brace to be killed in three or four hours. All parties were in earnest in keeping poachers away and the result was as I have stated. This shows what labourers can do if they like and what they will do if it is made in their interest to do so. They are either a great evil or a great boon to the game preserver and he must make up his mind either to have them as warm friends or bitter enemies.

'The regular and systematic poacher is a formidable fellow, opposed to all law and making a living the best way he can. After a time nothing comes amiss to him and though at first he has taken to his trade for a love of sport, it has ended in his adhering to it through necessity since he cannot get work when his character is known, for no man going poaching at night, can be fit for work in the day also.

'The existence and career of the poacher is the great drawback to the sportsman and it almost justifies the strong desire which so many hold to do away entirely with all game in order to get rid also of the tendency to poach. This is a question upon which I will not enter as it concerns the legislator more than the sportsman. At present the law permits the preservation of game and I believe that the evils attendant upon it are more than counterbalanced by its many advantages. As good subjects, therefore, we have only to avoid encouraging the poacher and the plan I have proposed in making it in the labourer's interest to discourage it is most humane as well as successful.

'Of regular poachers there are four chief varieties, viz first the systematic London poacher; 2nd the poaching gent; 3rd the regular rural poacher; 4th the poaching labourer.

'THE LONDON POACHER
. . . is almost always one of a gang and they conduct their operations in various ways. Sometimes they scour the country in dog carts drawn by a fast horse by which they are enabled to shoot from the sides of the road, either in covert or by catching pheasants on their feed or by beating the stubbles and turnips adjacent to the road or even invading the moors. As soon as a keeper or other person approaches, they take to their heels and on reaching the dog cart are soon out of sight. It is against these men that the regular

labourer may be most useful. Few farms in the shooting season are without a labourer within a field or two of every point likely to be invaded. Let everyone of these be provided with a railway whistle and let him blow it loudly as soon as he sees a suspicious person in the vicinity. This may be heard for a mile or more and the keeper may very soon be made aware of what is going on, besides, the whistle itself alarms the poacher as it proves a good system of watching and he prefers moving off to quieter quarters.

'These men generally travel in parties of five of whom one remains with the horse and their other four together surround a small covert and command every side so that a dog put in is sure to drive everything either to one or another of them or else take each side of the road, in the stubble, turnips etc. In this way a heavy load of game is soon bagged by these rascals by selecting a line of road studded with preserves and suited to their purpose. By keeping within the number of five they avoid the penalties of the 32nd section of the Game Laws and only come under the 30th and 31st section if they should be overtaken by a keeper and can only be fined £2 each. They seldom indulge in night poaching but are always ready to deal with the local poachers for the game which they may take in that way.

'THE POACHING GENT

. . . is generally a man who is ardently fond of shooting and yet has not the opportunity of indulging his appetite for sport from want of land to shoot over. He therefore is constantly trespassing upon the lands of his neighbours and of course subjects himself to the penalty of £2 on conviction of each offence. He is almost always, however, so good a shot that the produce of his gun enables him to pay this sum because he is so wary as to choose his opportunity and often escape detection for a considerable time. He knows where he is least likely to be caught, and the times which will suit him best and acts accordingly.

'There is seldom much difficulty in dealing with these men, and the harm they do in well preserved districts is very trifling. It is only on half preserved farms that they are to be dreaded and there they often get the lion's share of the spoil. On the grouse moors an inferior grade of this class is very destructive to game – he is the sporting miner or blacksmith or perhaps the denizen of some neighbouring small town in which he ought to be standing at the counter of some whisky shop or very often he is a shoemaker or tailor. These men are not regular night poachers but they are infected with a love of sport, to gratify which they brave all dangers and encounter even the risk of county jail.

'They wait for a day until the keepers are engaged in some particular direction and then by means of keeping on the sides of particular hills or other means suitable to the country, they are enabled to shoot an enormous quantity of grouse.

'THE REGULAR RURAL POACHER

. . . is the chief bane to the sport for though the London hand is very successful occasionally, he does not often pay more than one or two visits to the same preserve whilst the rural one is always on the lookout. It requires nearly as many keepers and watchers as there are poachers to be quite safe against their incursions, and even then if a watch is put upon every known man in the neighbourhood they will outwit you by giving intelligence to some distant friends in the same trade. They pursue their plans partly by day and partly by night.

'If by day their plan is to select a small covert which has just been visited by the keeper for whose round the poacher has long been waiting in concealment, then as soon as he is out of sight the poacher sets his wires and nets in a very few minutes and enters and disturbs the coppice either with or without a dog taught to run mute. In five minutes every hare is caught and quickly disposed of in some secret spot, often a labourer's cottage, until nightfall.

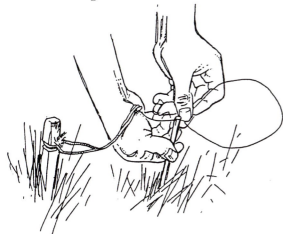

'In this way also a few pheasants are taken but not so easily as the hares as they do not run so easily as the latter and if sufficiently roused to do this some one or more are sure to give notice to the keepers in the distance by flying off to another covert which of itself is sufficient to arouse suspicion.

'At night the tricks of the regular poacher are most ingenious and are constantly varying in proportion to the discoveries of keepers. In moonlight and on dark windy nights the poacher's harvest is made. He can then see his game without so distinctly being heard as he would be on a quiet evening. He shoots the pheasants on their perches either with an air gun or fowling piece which is made to take to pieces easily for the convenience of putting in the pocket.

'Grouse and partridge are chiefly netted but the former may more easily be shot with an air gun at night since the net is much interfered with in consequence of the heather preventing its acting. The poacher however has no difficulty with either if he can only guess pretty nearly where they are and this he takes care to do by watching them with a glass at the close of evening. After taking his bearings at that time he is enabled to drop his net over the place without the trouble of using a stalking horse or the wide drag net.

'The only certain prevention against netting is to watch the birds at night and disperse them but this makes them so wild as to spoil subsequent shooting. Bushing the fields interferes with the drag net but not the bag net. It is a very good plan to go round every evening just before the calling of the birds and put a small bush or even with a spade

throw a lot of fresh earth on the last night's place of rest which is known by the droppings. This prevents their settling near the same spot which they would otherwise do, especially grouse. The poacher takes advantage of this fact by noting their droppings by day in order to find their settling place at night.

'Hares are taken by gate nets in the fields or by wires and bag nets in the coverts. It is a very remarkable fact that these cautious animals rarely use a hedge meuse at night preferring the gateways apparently from a fear of being surprised by the stoat or fox whilst by day the reverse is the case. The poacher cannot take them on the feed with a wire except in going in or out of the covert, but has recourse to the gate net which he fixes to the gate between the feeding field (usually a piece of swedes or clover) and the covert, then sending a mute running dog into the field he waits for the coming of the hare into the net and takes them out as fast as they run into it.

'There is no certain way of avoiding this mode of poaching excepting by careful watching. The chief guide is the scream of the hare when caught which may be hard on quiet nights but it is a practice very easily pursued by the poacher with little fear of detection if he is a clever and experienced hand.

'A practice has lately been introduced of setting wires in the runs made in the middle of feeding fields. It requires a wire to be set very carefully at a certain height by means of a twig and is very destructive. It is also very difficult to detect but as the poachers cannot find them except in very open moonlit nights, the keeper knows when to have his eyes open.

'THE POACHING LABOURER

. . . is a perfect pest to the parish in which he resides. He is constantly committing breaches of trust and does so at little risk and may escape detection for a long time. These men generally have a little terrier which is capable of being taught to do everything except speak and assists in a wonderful degree in the capture of game. They also have an old gun which takes apart easily and may be concealed under a smock frock. If a covey of birds is seen to collect near the cottage a slight noise is made and up go their heads at which moment the gun goes off and they are all dead at one swoop. The cottage is generally near the road so if a gun is heard some hedge-popping boy is made to bear the blame.

'Again these men generally have small gardens in which are parsley, pinks etc. which are a favourite food for the hare. She is almost sure to visit them and in her passage through the garden fence of course makes a meuse or at all events she leaves her mark or prick in the soil. If she goes through the gate this leads to her destruction the next night by wire, gin or net and no-one can possibly prevent it with the eyes of Argus.

'Pheasants also are sure to come within their reach occasionally and if they do they may be wired easily enough. A man for instance is put to hedging or draining and is on the ground by six o'clock in the morning, a time when pheasants have not left their feed, and he has only to lay a few horsehair loops along the ditches and by gently driving the pheasants into them, apparently in the course of his work, he captures every now and then the value of a day's work in a few minutes. Of course he conceals the booty until night.

* * *

'Such are the most common tricks of poachers, but the most successful are those who invent plans of their own. The keeper has enough to do to outwit them and his grand

object should be to find out their plan and circumvent it – then it is diamond cut diamond. A reformed poacher, if really reformed, makes the best keeper but unfortunately for this purpose their exposure to night air and to wet and cold and their habits of intemperance have almost always destroyed their constitutions before they think of reforming. It is only when worn out as poachers that they think of turning round and becoming keepers.

'When the head keeper is really up to his business the poachers stand a very poor chance, especially if the master is ready to support the servant with his influence and protection. In every case, whether on the open moors or in enclosed districts, the first thing to be done is to make a list of all the poachers likely to visit your manor, then discover their habits and haunts and the kind of game they excel in taking. Next get some steady, hardy and useful watchers, if possible strangers to the locality and therefore not likely to be influenced by the ties of affinity or friendship.

'Let these men speedily make themselves conversant with the appearance of all poachers on your manor or your head keeper can initiate them by degrees. They should all have glasses and be made conversant with their use for even on a comparatively small beat it often happens that a poacher cannot be approached within many hundred yards and yet it is quite impossible to speak with any certainty of a man's identity at a quarter of a mile.

'When these men know their duties pretty well, each should have one or more poachers allotted to him and should always be able to give an account of his whereabouts. He does this partly by his own powers of watching but chiefly from information gained from other parties. By such a mode of proceeding almost any gang of poachers may be outwitted. They seldom show fight when they find themselves no match in brain! though in personal prowess they may be superior. Intellect and pluck will always be served, even when mere brute force has totally failed.'

· THE GAME LAWS ·

It was said often and bitterly that the Game Laws were concocted and imposed by those who owned the game in the first place and who also sat upon the bench in judgement of malefactors. The modern Game Laws have their roots in the 1831 legislation which was unequivocal about its views of poachers and poaching and imposed heavy penalties for transgressors.

This is a contemporary abstract given by 'Stonehenge' of the Game Laws which were upheld with such vigour in the Victorian era and which underpinned the age-old conflict between poacher, keeper and landowner.

'By these Acts persons taking or destroying game at night, viz from an hour after sunset to an hour before sunrise shall be committed for the first offence for three months, second offence six months to hard labour and find sureties afterwards. For a third offence liable to be transported. Owners and occupiers, lords of the manor or their servants may apprehend, and if violent resistance is made it shall be a misdemeanour and may be punished with transportation for seven years or two years imprisonment.

'Three persons entering land armed with the purpose of taking game shall be guilty of misdemeanour and punishable by imprisonment or transportation. The Act extends to taking unlawfully any game or rabbits by night on any public road, highway or path or the sides thereof or at the openings, outlets or gates from any such land into any such public road, highway or path. 'Game' to include hares, pheasants, partridges, heath or moor game, black game or bustards.

'Any person killing or taking game or using a gun, dog or net or engine for that purpose on a Sunday or Christmas Day is subject on conviction by two Justices to a penalty not exceeding £5 and costs.

'Persons licensed to deal in game who shall buy or sell or have in their possession any bird of game after ten days, and persons unlicensed who shall buy or sell any bird of game (except such as are kept in any breeding places or mews) shall be subject on conviction before two Justices to a penalty not exceeding £1 for every head of game.

'Persons killing or taking game or using any gun, dog etc. for the purpose of searching for game without Game Certificate are subject to a penalty not exceeding £5 as well as the penalty under the Game Certificate Act. Any person not having the right of killing game on land or permission from the person having such right who shall wilfully take or destroy on such land the eggs or any bird of game, wild duck, swan, teal or widgeon or shall knowingly have in his possession any eggs so taken, shall pay a sum not exceeding 5 shillings for every egg, with costs. Persons not licensed to deal in game, buying game from unlicensed persons subject to a penalty not exceeding £5 with costs.

'Persons trespassing in the daytime in search of game, woodcocks, snipes, quails, landrails or conies may, on conviction by one Justice be fined not exceeding £2 with costs and the lease of the occupier if not entitled to the game shall not be a sufficient defence against the landlord.

'Trespassers may be required to quit and to tell their names and abode and in case of refusal may be arrested and on conviction before one Justice may be fined not exceeding £5. But the party arrested must be discharged unless brought before a Justice within twelve hours, though he may even thereby, be afterwards summoned.

'In case five or more persons enter upon land and shall by violence and menace endeavour to prevent any authorised person from approaching with the purpose of requiring them to quit or tell their names or places of abode, each person shall be fined not exceeding £5 with costs. Penalties for trespassers not to extend to persons hunting or coursing and being in fresh pursuit of any deer, hare or fox already started. Game may be taken from trespassers who shall refuse to deliver up the same.

'Penalties to be paid to overseers of the parish, one half to go to the use of the county and the other to the informer. Imprisonment in the case of non payment.

'No owner or occupier to have power to grant permission to more than one person at the same time in each parish to take hares, such authority or a copy thereof to be delivered to the Clerk of the Magistrates.'

Thus we have a system stitched up tightly to ensure that the squire's game was protected at all times day and night from unauthorised human predation. A fine of £5 was equivalent to at least a month's wages for a farm labourer and you may be sure that only in rare cases would the culprit have instant access to such a sum for a fine, far less a defence lawyer, so that imprisonment was the most likely outcome of a successful prosecution.

The critical number of five persons constituting a gang was closely observed – and usually avoided – by the poachers: to enter land in pursuit of game 'mob-handed' brought heavier penalties than a group of four or fewer; thus canny poachers made sure that they came alone or in small numbers – although this did not deter those who deliberately came with a small army to confront the keepers and raid the coverts.

Mention of the likes of landrails (corncrakes), bustards and quails implies that those birds were to be encountered a century and a half ago, whereas today they are extinct in the UK or only hanging on in tiny numbers.

There was no chink through which a poacher might penetrate the legislation, no legal loophole he might exploit. His favoured methods to include all 'engines' were mentioned particularly, and day and night offences were dealt with separately, with more severe penalties for offences carried out under cover of darkness, also Sundays and Christmas Day: stealing eggs, selling out of season and even taking a pot-shot from the public highway were all identified and firmly blocked.

Rarely can such a piece of legislation have been so carefully researched and vigorously applied, for the self-interest of the landowners whose property was being preserved ensured blanket, comprehensive, thorough and absolute protection for their sport. We note that when in hot pursuit of fox or hare the rules did not apply; but then, only the squire and the well-to-do went hunting – it was not a sport for the poaching fraternity.

Those laws are the basis of the current Game Laws, the shooting seasons, rules about Sunday shooting, night poaching, poaching mob-handed and game dealing which apply to this day. The major change has been in the level of punishment, which the shooting community considers far too lenient (although many, but by no means all, would stop short of deportation), while the townsfolk believe it to be just as Draconian as in the worst of the early Victorian days.

· VILLAGE LOYALTY ·

The clannish ways of village folk are food for thought for our latter-day, rather more selfish and acquisitive generation. In 1891 John Watson the poacher had a simple philosophy.

'We were taking many birds and game at this time. Some birds were undamaged and these we had stuffed and as for the rest – most were disposed of in the village and greatly helped to relieve the hardship which was rampant consequent on the lack of employment. I would like to suggest to my listeners a piece of the Scriptures which runs "It is more blessed to give than to receive".

'To experience real privation is to learn the lesson and if one is in a position to relieve matters by providing a hare, a couple of rabbits, a chicken or a joint they will be gladly received. The way to give a good gift is not to do it with a blare of trumpets or a banging of the door but just an unostentatious opening of the door and thrusting the gift inside and not waiting for any thanks. One doesn't lose by this method. There are no questions asked and no explanations given.

'This is the way country folk used to help each other in times of stress. Sometimes it was a salmon, sometimes a hare, sometimes birds. No wonder the whole village petitioned for the release of the best poacher from the claws of injustice. They called us "clannish" but such a spirit of helpfulness if extended o'er all the earth would turn people into one large clan and the world would be the better for it.'

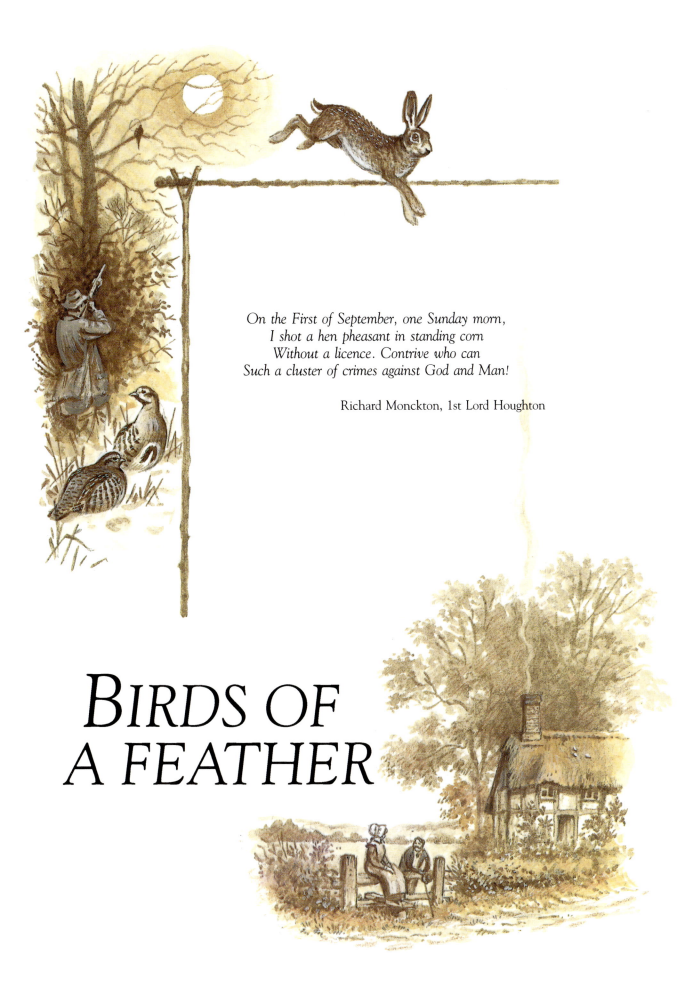

On the First of September, one Sunday morn,
I shot a hen pheasant in standing corn
Without a licence. Contrive who can
Such a cluster of crimes against God and Man!

Richard Monckton, 1st Lord Houghton

BIRDS OF
A FEATHER

No book on poaching would be complete without an extract from the great classic The
Amateur Poacher *(1878) by that delightful but troubled country writer, Richard
Jefferies, writing a century ago of times changed but of many things in the sporting
field which have remained constant. Here is one of my favourite episodes of how the
two boys, Jefferies himself and his friend 'Orion', hunt the fields of Farmer Willum
who is plagued at the intrusions and poaching of the neighbouring keepers who beat
his ground, knowing that he is too infirm to see them off. Thus the biter is truly bit.
This is a wonderfully told, minor classic of the shooting field.*

*Farmer Willum had made no changes to his farm and it was as it had been a
hundred years before, somewhere in the middle of the eighteenth century. The thatch,
whitewash, swallows' nests and even the besom left by the door with which visitors
might brush the mud from their boots before entering the parlour, paint a charming
picture of rustic times past.*

'The morning we had chosen was fine and after shaking hands with Farmer Willum whose
shooting days were over, we entered the lane and by it the fields. The meadows were
small, enclosed with double mounds and thickly timbered so that as the ground was level,
you could not see beyond the field in which you stood, and upon looking over the gate
might surprise a flock of pigeons, a covey of partridges or a rabbit out feeding. Though the
tinted leaves were falling fast, the hedges were still full of plants and vegetation that
prevented seeing through them. The "kuck-kuck" of the redwings came from the bushes,
the first notes of approaching Winter. Red haws on the hawthorn and hips on the briar
sprinkled the hedge with bright spots of colour.

'The two spaniels went with such an eager rush into the thick double mound, dashing
heedlessly through the nettles and under the brambles that we hastened to get on each

side of the hedge. A rustling – a short bark,
another, then a movement among the rushes
in the ditch, evidently not made by the dogs,
and then a silence. But the dogs came back
and as they give tongue, a rabbit rushes past
a bare spot on the slope of the bank. I fire –
a snap shot – and cut out some fur but do no
further harm, the pellets bury themselves in
the earth. But startled and perhaps stung by
a stray shot, the rabbit bolts fairly at least
twenty yards in front of Orion with the
spaniel tearing at his heels.

'Up goes the double barrel with a bright
gleam as the sunlight glances on it. A second
of suspense then from the black muzzle darts a
cylinder of tawny flame and an opening cone
of white smoke; a sharp report rings on the
ear. The rabbit rolls over and over and is dead
before the dog can seize it. After harling the
rabbit, Orion hangs him high on a projecting
branch so that the man who is following us at
a distance may easily find the game.

'We then tried a corner where two of these large mounds meeting, formed a small copse in which grew a quantity of withy and the thick grasses that always border the stoles. A hare bolted almost directly the dogs went in: hares trust in their speed, rabbits in doubling for cover. I fired right and left and missed, fairly missed with both barrels. Orion jumped on the mound from the other side and from that elevation sent a third cartridge after her.

'It was a long, a very long shot but the hare perceptibly winced. Still she drew away easily from the dogs, going straight for a distant gateway. But before it was reached the pace slackened, she made ineffectual attempts to double as the slow spaniels overtook her but her strength was ebbing and they quickly ran in. Reloading and in none of the best of tempers I followed the mound. The miss was of course the gun's fault – it was foul, or the cartridges, or the bad quality of the powder.

* * *

'The spaniels plunged in the brook among the flags but though they made a great splashing nothing came of it till we approached a marshy place where there was a pond. A moorhen then rose and scuttled down the brook, her legs dragging along the surface some distance before she could get up and the sunshine sparkled from the water that fell from her. I fired and knocked her over: at the sound of the discharge a bird rose from the low mound by the pond some forty yards ahead. My second barrel was empty in an instant.

'Both Orion's followed but the distance, the intervening pollard willows and our excitement spoilt the aim. The woodcock flew off untouched and made straight away from the territories we could beat into those that were jealously guarded by a certain keeper with whom Farmer Willum had waged war for years. "Come on!" shouted Orion as soon as he had marked the cock down in a mound two fields away. Throwing him my gun I leaped the brook and we at first raced but on second thoughts walked slowly for the mound. Running disturbs accuracy of fire, and a woodcock was much too rare a visitor for the slightest chance to be lost.

'As we approached we considered that very probably the cock would either lie close till we had walked past or he would get up behind out of gunshot. What we were afraid of was his making for the preserves which were not far off. So we tossed for the best position and I lost. I had therefore to get over on the side of the hedge towards the preserves and to walk down somewhat faster than Orion who was to keep on his side about thirty yards behind. The object was to flush the cock on his side so that if he missed, the bird might return towards our territories. In a double mound like this it is impossible to tell what a woodcock will do, but this was the best thing we could think of.

'About half way down the hedge I heard Orion fire both barrels in quick succession, the mound was so thick I could not see through. The next instant the cock came over the top of the hedge just above my head. Seeing me so close he flew straight along the summit of the bushes, a splendid chance to look from a distance, but throwing up the gun, a projecting briar caught the barrels and before I could recover it, the bird came down at the side of the hedge.

'It was another magnificent chance but again three pollard willows interfered and as I fired the bark flew off one of them in small strips. Quickened by the whistling pellets, the cock suddenly lifted himself again to the top of the hedge to go over and for a moment came into full view and quite fifty yards away. I fired snap shot as a forlorn hope and lost sight of him but the next instant I heard Orion call, "He's down!". One single chance pellet had dropped the cock, he fell on the other side just under the hedge.

'We hastened back to the brook thinking that the shooting would attract the keepers and did not stay to look at the bird until safe over the water. The long beak, the plumage that seems painted almost in the exact tints of the dead brown leaves he loves so well, the eyes large by comparison and so curiously placed towards the poll of his head as if to see behind him – there was not a point that did not receive its share of admiration. We shot about half a dozen rabbits, two more hares and a wood pigeon afterwards, but all these were nothing compared with the woodcock.

'How Farmer Willum chuckled over it, specially to think that we had cut out the game from under the very batteries of the enemy. It was the one speck of bitterness in the old man's character – his hatred of this keeper. Disabled himself by age and rheumatism from walking far he heard daily reports from his men of this fellow coming over the boundary to shoot or driving pheasant or partridge away. It was a sight to see Farmer Willum stretch his bulky length in his old arm chair, right before the middle of the great fire of logs on the hearth, twiddling his huge thumbs and every now and then indulging in a hearty laugh followed by a sip at the "straight cup".'

· RABBITY DICK ·

In his 1982 book Pennine Poacher (Dalesman Books) *Richard Fawcett introduces
the character of 'Rabbity Dick' who has a nasty scare one night when after pheasants,
an experience which might have had lesser mortals running for their lives.*

'I got a heck of a fright in the wood somewhere around 4.30 one Sunday morning just in
the New Year 1941, I believe. The birds would be much scarcer than two months before.
I had squared my mates to let me get away by 4.0am "home to my bed", but actually a
brace of pheasants was my motive. There was quite a full moon but it was well on its way
downhill. I walked up one ride quietly peering about, stopping to listen every few minutes.
I had no dog with me this time. Wandering along the paths I came upon, here and there,
a feed hopper with grain for the birds. I was keeping out of the rough undergrowth.

'Eventually I came to the point where the path forked in two directions each side of
a large holly tree which still stands there. I had moved round to the semi-moonlit side of

the tree to shine my torch inside and around it when there, only two feet from me, was a man in a trilby hat staring at me.

'I hadn't used the torch up to that point and nearly died with the sudden shock of it. I have escaped danger many times by taking to my heels and hiding and dodging, never having been caught. I have often told my friends that if ever I was caught red-handed with no hope of escape, I would not use violence. I would laugh and grin for to be caught would strike me as a great joke. And now it had happened!

'The man just stared at me, he never spoke so I said in a friendly voice, "How do!" He never answered or moved. I said something else – and there was still no reply from him. Still it would have been bad manners to shine the torch in his eyes. He looked like a dead man stood up. I could have been two hundred yards away by now, but the old beggar might have a gun. I knew everybody locally but I didn't know this one. This wasn't Wardie the keeper, so I reached forward and touched his face and nose – ice cold! I jumped back and shone my torch on him. And then I saw it was an old statue made of pot, stone or alabaster – Phew!

'I think I sat down by the side of him for company. I found out later that the owner of the wood had bought two garden ornaments some time previous. One was stood in the garden, the other in the wood as some sort of a joke. It certainly was no joke for me for a few seconds!'

· BIRD-CATCHING IN THE ·
SEVENTEENTH CENTURY

In 1686 Richard Blome's book The Gentleman's Recreation, *described some sure-fire ways of taking various birds without resorting to powder and shot.*

'A Way to take PIGEONS and CROWS or ROOKS, very pleasant.

'Take some thick brown paper cut a sheet into about 8 parts and make them up like sugar loaves, then lime the inside of the paper indifferent well three or four days before you intend to set them. Then put into each paper towards the further end two or three grains of corn, lie these papers on the ground as near as you can to some clods of earth, early in the morning before they come to feed. The quantity you may use at your discretion, the more the better, about a hundred is indifferent.

'When they come to feed they will espy the corn and begin to peck them out by thrusting in the head; then are they hoodwinked for they can't get it off by reason it sticks close to their feathers. When they find themselves thus served they take wing and will fly bolt upright until, they have spent themselves and then come tumbling down to the delight of the Spectators.

'To Take WATERFOWL.

'Take the seeds, leaves and roots of the Herb called Bellenge, and having cleansed from them all filth, put them in a vessel of clean running water and let them lie seeping therein at least twenty four hours and then boil them in the said water until it is almost consumed. Then take it off the fire let it cool and scatter it in such places where the fowl have their haunts. They will greedily eat it so that they become immediately intoxicated and lie in a Trance as if dead. But you must watch them, for the fumes will soon wear off.

'Some do add to this concoction the Powder of Brimstone boiled therein, which is very effectual.

'To Take LANDFOWL.

'Take a peck of lesser quantity of Wheat, Rye, Barley, Pease or Tares, to which put two or three handfuls of Nux-Vomica and boil them in Running Water, very well until they are almost ready to burst. Then take it off the fire and when they are cold strew them on the land where you design to take the fowl and such that eat thereof will immediately be intoxicated and lie as if dead so that they may be taken up at pleasure provided you stay not too long (for the dizziness will not last long upon them, therefore be near at hand).

'If you approve not of Nux Vomica or Lees of Wine you may infuse the said Grains or Seeds in the juice of Hemlock mixing therein the Seeds of Henbane and Poppy or either of them.'

· NETTING PARTRIDGES ·

This account of netting partridges by an anonymous poacher of 1880 shows a novel way of counteracting the popular counter measure used by keepers of 'bushing the fields':

'Netting partridges always requires two persons, though a third to walk behind the net is helpful. If the birds have been carefully marked down, a narrow net is used; if their roosting place is uncertain, a wider net is better. When all is ready this is slowly dragged along the ground and is dropped immediately the whirr or wings is heard. If neatly and silently done the whole covey is bagged. There is a wild flutter, a cloud of brown feathers and all is over.

'It is not always, however, that the draw is so successful. In view of preventing this method of poaching, especially on land where many partridges roost, keepers plant low, scrubby thorns at intervals. These so far interfere with the working of the net as to allow the birds time to escape. We were never much troubled, though, in this way. As opportunity offered the quick thorns were torn up and dead black thorn boughs took their place. As the thorns were low the difference was never noticed even by the keepers, and of course they were carefully removed before and replaced after netting. Even when the dodge was detected, the fields and fallows had been pretty well stripped of the birds. This method is impractical now as the modern method of reaping leaves the stubble as bare as the squire's lawn.

'We had always a great objection to use a wide net where a narrow one would suit the purpose. Among turnips and where large numbers of birds were supposed to lie, a number of rows or "rigs" were taken at a time until the whole of the ground had been traversed. This last method is one that requires time and a knowledge of the keeper's beat. On rough ground the catching of the net may be obviated by having about eighteen inches of calico bordering the lowest and trailing part of it.'

31

· NETTING FRENCH PARTRIDGES ·

Brian Vesey Fitzgerald writes of poaching and poaching ways in his charming little book It's My Delight *(Eyre & Spottiswoode, 1947), which all students of the subject should read. In this extract he describes a way of netting French partridges in a manner other than the traditional trail-net, a dodge which takes advantage of the bird's preference for running rather than flying from danger. This is another instance which shows the amazing sagacity and usefulness of the well trained lurcher.*

'French partridges may be netted . . . and with equal success. But the Frenchman is often taken by gypsies in another and simpler way. The French partridge, as every shooting man knows, is a lazy bird and is most averse to taking wing if it can possibly avoid doing so. There is, therefore, no need to go to the trouble of walking with a net. It is much easier and every bit as certain to get the birds to walk into the net. This can be done with the aid of two or three well trained dogs.

'The birds must be watched into their roosting place and the lie of the land from the place must be carefully noted. The net must be set downwind from the birds and the dog must be put in upwind from the birds. The process is in fact exactly the reverse from that of walking them with the net. The reasons are twofold. Firstly the birds must scent the dogs and secondly they must not find anything to encourage them to take to wing. Birds, like aeroplanes, prefer to take off into the wind. But the wind in this case means into the dogs, and the French partridge would always prefer to run if that is the case. Furthermore they are not sure that there is really any danger. They will not move until the dogs are almost on top of them and then they start to run away from the dogs but not too fast, for they are not sure if the dogs are really after them and they do not want to go too far from the roost if there is not really any need to do so.

'Two well trained lurchers are sufficient to do the job thoroughly, but three are better for then there is less chance of any birds running out. I have seen some remarkable dog work done by a team of lurchers for that matter. Not least remarkable has been the way in which the dogs have refused to be distracted by hares and rabbits which they may have put up on the way to the net. Yet the same dogs may be used the next night for hares. How they are trained in this manner and to this state of perfection I do not yet know but I hope to find out some day. At any rate, the Gypsy's lurcher seems to understand exactly what it is required to do on a partridge night just as he understands what is required on a hare night.'

· RABBITY DICK TAKES GROUSE ·

'Rabbity Dick' of North Yorkshire, whom we have already introduced (p28), used his job as a railwayman as a wonderful platform for his poaching. His local knowledge was encyclopaedic and only once does he record being lost on the moors. Grouse poaching is not common but Dick liked the taste of grouse and made a point of shooting a few each season as much for devilment as anything. On this occasion he decided to celebrate the Glorious Twelfth and walk the moors for a quick shot before the posh shooting party arrived later in the day. He took his 20-bore, a game bag, ten cartridges and his little dog, and his only protection from the weather was a gaberdine mac. Thus he settles down for the night ready for an early start, not to know that the experience was one he was to remember all his life:

'I snuggled tightly into my little sitting-up couch of heather. It was a perfect August night in the middle of an unusually hot spell of weather. It had been very hot on the Sunday, tomorrow promised to be hotter. It never really did get dark. It was wonderfully warm and I did not get one slight shiver all night. Old Ingleborough was silhouetted against a clear sky almost opposite me but a long way off due north. To the west was a kind of golden pink sky and to the east the promise of an early dawn. Two or three miles away I could see a stretch of the moorland road. Never a light passed along that road while I sat there. All around I could hear grouse muttering and grunting in their sleep.

'By 3.30 the whole moor was like a wonderland to me. The cock grouse were on the move, crowing and cackling in all directions. By 4.30 the sky to the east was beginning to lighten. The day was going to be a scorcher. And as the sky began to lighten, even a little bit, the grouse literally went delirious with joy. Cock birds by the hundred were crowing all over the moor, throwing themselves up in the air anything from two feet to

ten and fluttering back onto their own private tussock or small hill. What a long playing record I could have got of their song that morning, "Harr Harr; Go Back, Go Back;" they were calling. One old cock only two feet from my right ear jumped and bounced with excitement for a good twenty minutes until I stealthily made a grab for his legs. Then he made off "Harr-harring" at me. I sounded my "Harr-Harr" and "Bah-Bah" at him and he or another one was back within minutes.

'I could have had at least five brace of grouse from my hideout, but that was not my policy. There was no fun shooting a grouse on the ground at any time and definitely not on a morning like this when the world around me was teeming and bubbling with their excitement. But all these cheerful and happy birds around me had not a lot to crow about if they had only known. Before the day was out there would be hundreds of them shot dead and a lot of others would be severely damaged by stray pellets hitting them.

'I rose from my couch at around 5.10am and set off smartly east. The keeper wouldn't have slept a wink that night. Most of them don't the night before the first shoot. He might cruise up the road in his car to see that all was well, which is why I always give myself a mile start.

'Within two hundred yards I had four birds with four shots. Not bad doing; I have enough. I have broken my duck and it is bad "keeping" weather. They will be fly-blown before I get home. I packed them into my bag and emptied my gun. "Come on Trixie", I said and then struck off straight in an easterly direction at my usual Cumberland "Lang Gallop", a good swinging pace especially if I was going "In Bank" (downhill). I wanted to be well clear of the moors before the sun got right into my eyes. I could see he wouldn't be long looking over the top of me. Then down through the pastures and green lanes and home some time before 8.0am.

'I had walked maybe ten miles since my night's lodge. In that distance I had never looked back once to see if anyone was after me. I had not any need to do so. My instinct would have told me if there had been. Yes, I could easily have got ten brace; I was well satisfied with two. And nothing can take the memory of that night away now – I have written it down. Going to work on the night of that 12th August I heard that more than 200 brace of grouse had been shot. That could mean 500 birds dead.'

· POACHING AT SANDRINGHAM ·

This extract from the classic by Colin Willock, Kenzie The Wild Goose Man (André Deutsch, 1962), tells of one of the greatest latter-day poachers, the late Mackenzie Thorpe of Sutton Bridge in Lincolnshire. The very good friend of Peter Scott, wildfowler, boxer and artist, 'Kenzie' has become one of the folk heroes of our sport in spite of his nefarious activities which more often than not put him outside the law. Colin has kindly allowed me to tell a couple of the yarns from his famous work, one of the better books about our sport which should be on every bookshelf.

In this, the first episode I shall recount, Kenzie and his friend Horry Savage had decided to poach nothing less than the royal estate at Sandringham: Kenzie was nothing if not ambitious. They had shot one cock pheasant from the car window and were waiting for the evening when the birds would go up to roost, when an official-looking Land Rover came down the lane and blocked their exit.

' "Leave this to me", Kenzie told Horry.

'Two men jumped out of the Land Rover, one a big, elderly fellow and the other much younger. There was no doubt who they were and what they wanted. These were the royal keepers.

"Hullo," said the big man; "what's your business?"

"Can you tell me", countered Kenzie, "whether this is the right road for Sandringham?"

"You don't have to ask that, do you?" said the big man. "We're going to search the car."

"You can't," said Kenzie, "you're not constables, you're just keepers." It was a good legal point but not, apparently, good enough, for the older man said, "I'm Mr Amos, the King's head keeper and I'm also a police constable."

'Kenzie was now sure that the game was up. All he wanted to do was to save the guns, particularly the .22 rifle which he still held between his knees. He played for time. "Can I see your identity card as a constable?" he asked Amos. While the keeper was producing it, Kenzie climbed out of the Austin and dropped the .22 rifle in the long grass. Unfortunately there was not quite enough grass to cover it. The younger keeper had by now found the .410 under the front seat but hadn't come across the cock pheasant.

'Kenzie grabbed the gun and said, "You can't take that. We ain't been poaching." He threw the .410 back into the car. The keepers had not yet found any evidence of poaching and there was still, in Kenzie's view, time to make a getaway. With luck Horry could just edge past the Land Rover. "Come on," he ordered Horry; "let's get out of it."

'But this time the Austin 7 would not start. Worse, the keepers had spotted the rifle lying in the grass. Kenzie jumped out of the car and dived at it. The keepers dived too, and all three were on the ground with a hold on the gun. They fought for several seconds and then the younger keeper let go and jumped on Kenzie's back. At this Kenzie released Amos and the rifle to throw off his assailant. Amos unopposed now had the rifle and the battle was lost.

'Considering the set-to they parted amicably enough, but the summonses arrived for Kenzie and Horry as usual. The bill . . . included confiscation of a rifle, £1 for possession of a firearm without certificate, £5 for coming from land in pursuit of game, £4 for trespassing and £1 for opposing a constable.

'Even now Kenzie still complains of the injustice of certain aspects of the affair. "Amos" he says bitterly, "was not a constable; he was only a *special* constable." '

· TROUBLE WITH TRIP WIRES ·

Harold Wyman in The Great Game *(Fieldfare Books) describes his trouble with trip wires and learns that it is possible to raid the same place just once too often:*

'Some years ago I was particularly attracted to a certain covert in Shropshire and, familiarity which breeds contempt almost became my undoing as I became careless, shooting the above mentioned covert on a Monday and Tuesday nights, bagging 32 brace on the first occasion and 25 and a half on the second. Returning once more on the Wednesday we entered the same covert and were confronted by a lit lantern in the release pen. This was an obvious indication of the keepers' knowledge of our visits and remembering Thomas Moor's advice about such keepers being afraid to tackle the intruder, we decided to walk the main ride. Caution being the watch word I held a light stick low in front and it was but a few paces before the stick located a trip wire which stretched across the ride knee high. This wire was fastened to a slide bar which, when released by an intruder, dropped and detonated a cartridge. This was safely negotiated as were a few more. Sixteen brace were shot and we escaped unscathed.

'Choosing a night of wind and rain to make our fourth and final effort to wrest longtails from the estate, even though we were aware that the keeper was now fully alert to our visits, we entered the wood and moved along the ride as we did on the previous occasion, feeling my way by making use of a thin stick. The keeper however, was far more crafty than we credited him with being. The trip wires had been moved further along the ride and the height varied in an attempt to lull us into a sense of false security thinking the wires had been removed, but we had been underestimated and after locating and passing over or under four trips we eventually arrived among our quarry.

'They were unusually spooky despite the wind and rain that favoured our activity. On occasion three or four cock birds left the roost as we advanced, each giving an alarm call. Needless to say I am never at ease in a covert when such conditions prevail. Every pheasant was put on the alert and we were lucky to bag eight brace. Uneasy and disappointed with the results obtained, I decided to carry the birds already shot out of the covert and plant them in a ditch a field away, a wise precaution it turned out to be, in view of the alarming performance of the cock birds.

'Re-entering the covert we turned off into a ride not yet exploited by us and almost walked into the trap which could well have been nemesis for my companion and I, but thanks to the inexperience of our ambushers we eluded capture. Instead of allowing us to walk right into the trap, our adversaries suddenly switched on their lamps and charged from a distance of fifteen to twenty yards. We were not caught napping. Instantly reacting to the situation we turned and sprinted for the main ride. Entering this and running along it for fifty yards we spotted the tell-tale white markers we had attached to the first few trip wires, taking them in our stride.

'My companion being younger and fleeter of foot than I, was ten yards ahead and he completely misjudged the last wire. Hitting it at top speed he was still airborne when the roar of the alarm gun blended with the wind and rain. We were leaving a shambles in our wake for a number of our pursuers had hit the wires and their cries of alarm were a welcome sound.

'Bouncing back like a rubber ball, my fallen ally had soon regained the few yards I had gained during his fall and was running alongside me chuckling gleefully at the confusion of our enemies. His grim demeanour soon returned when half way across the field where safety lay we saw the headlights of several vehicles turning into the estate and for the next hour it was a case of hide and seek. Finally we managed to slip safely away and returned just before dawn to collect our eight brace of birds without incident.

'We continued to poach that estate for many years after that eventful night, sometimes being forced by pressure from the keepers to move on, but returning a month or so later to practise the nocturnal art, never overdoing it because I was informed by a beater that the Guns were well pleased with the number of pheasants flying over them on shooting days.'

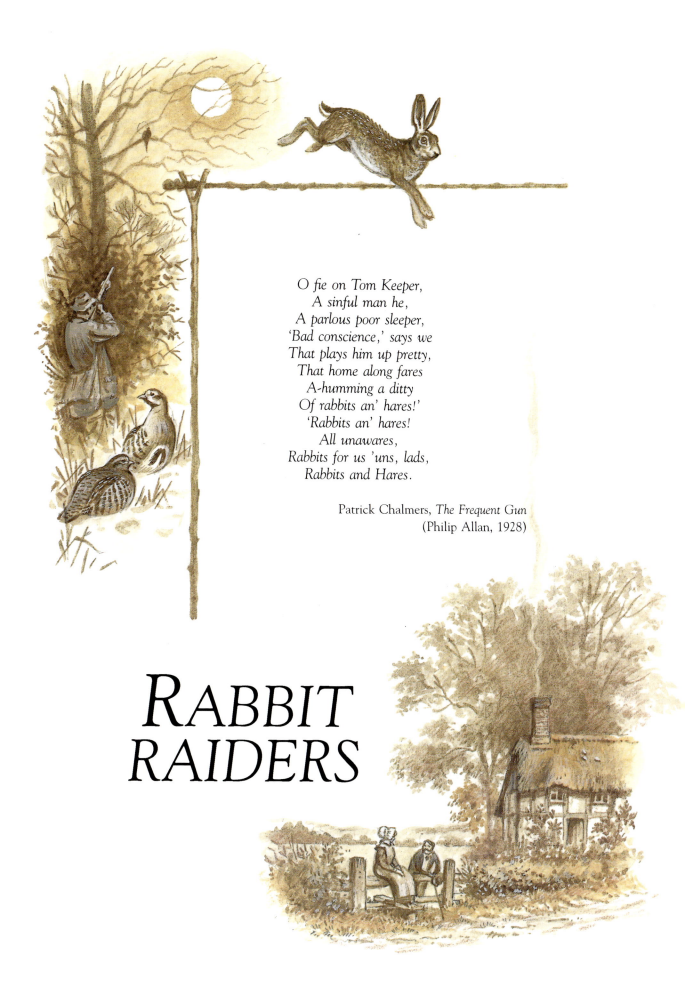

O fie on Tom Keeper,
A sinful man he,
A parlous poor sleeper,
'Bad conscience,' says we
That plays him up pretty,
That home along fares
A-humming a ditty
Of rabbits an' hares!'
'Rabbits an' hares!
All unawares,
Rabbits for us 'uns, lads,
Rabbits and Hares.

Patrick Chalmers, *The Frequent Gun*
(Philip Allan, 1928)

RABBIT RAIDERS

· SWINGEING GAME LAW PENALTIES ·

This extract, taken from The Sportsman's Dictionary (1907) *is an example of the Game Laws of 1792 and shows the swingeing penalties incurred by all those who took game illegally, while those who informed upon them often received the bulk of the fine. The £5 referred to would have been almost a year's wages for a peasant in those times, and a tempting inducement for the conviction of a neighbour. For a third offence the combination of a flogging, a £50 fine and imprisonment showed that those who owned the hares were keen to see that things stayed that way.*

'Every person tracing or coursing hares in the snow shall be committed for one year unless he pay the Churchwardens for the use of the poor, 20s for every hare or become bound by recognizances with two sureties in £20 a piece not to offend again. Every person taking or destroying hares with any sort of engine shall forfeit for every hare 20s.

'Unqualified persons keeping or using sporting dogs or engines to take or destroy hares shall forfeit £5 to the informer with double costs by distress or be committed for three months for a first offence and for every other, four months. Taking or killing a hare in the night time, forfeit £5, the whole to the informer with double costs. Killing or taking with gun, dog or engine, a hare in the night between the hours of seven at night and six in the morning from October 12th to February 12th or in the day time on Sunday or Christmas Day, to forfeit no less than £10, no more than £20 for the first offence, no less than £20 no more than £30 for the second offence and £50 for the third offence and upon neglect or refusal be committed for six to twelve months and may be publicly whipped.

'Persons armed and disguised stealing hens, higler, chapman, carrier, inn-keeper, victualler or alehouse keeper, having in his custody or buying or selling or offering to sell any hare unless sent by some person qualified, shall forfeit for every hare £5, the whole to the informer.'

· THE NETTER NETTED ·

Chippy Smith of Tamerton Foliot, Devon is a traditional old-timer and part-time keeper responsible for sending me a number of wonderful tales; he was involved in a lovely story, told in Poachers' Tales, *in which he and a pal fired the crazy muzzle-loader at a roosting pheasant, although now Chippy is pretty sure that it was, in fact, a flock of starlings. Now eighty years old he has been persuaded to send a couple of reminiscences, this one about a night with the long-net.*

'Many years ago we worked for the Air Ministry in the construction of a new airfield. We had access to a large area of fields and woods and were on good terms with the local farmers so we knew where the rabbits were lying out.

'Having a long-net at home I decided on my next weekend to bring it up and see if we could thin them out. My pal at the Ministry had never been long-netting before so we had a dry run in the day time to work it all out and explain the setting drill.

'On the night the wind was perfect for this particular wood. Having set the net I explained to my pal he had to go, dragging a tin full of small stones to move the rabbits. On his return to the net he would work from the far end taking out the rabbits and I would meet him half way along. The net was 150 yards long. All was ready so I whispered to him to set off and drive them in.

'I stayed at my end holding the top line waiting for the bumps which showed that rabbits were hitting the net. After about twenty minutes I heard a helluva noise and began to scan the skyline expecting to see a flock of bunnies making for the wood. It was my pal chasing straight towards the centre of the net with two large dray horses in hot pursuit of him.

'I started to shout "Mind the net!" but no use: he came on hell for leather towards the wood. He hit the net full tilt and ended up totally meshed, lying in the brambles while the two Shires just stood blowing and staring down at him.

'I said that he should have ignored them: they would not have hurt him. He replied that "With them bloody great feet they would have shoved me into the ground".

'Sad to say we did not pick up a single rabbit that night.'

· UGLY BUSINESS ·

The historian Trevelyan comments on the injustice of the later and equally cruel (1826) Law and of the trouble it was to cause in his book English Social History *(1942). He makes the distinction, in which he is not alone, between the humble cottager and the violent gangs from the towns.*

'By a new Law of 1816, the starving cottager who went out to take a hare or rabbit for the family pot could be transported for seven years if caught with the nets upon him at night. Less sympathy need be felt for bands of ruffians from towns who invaded the preserves and fought pitched battles, twenty a side, with shot guns at close range, against the gentlemen and gamekeepers who came out against them. The poaching war had become a very ugly business.'

· DETERRING THE HARE NETTERS ·

'Old Velveteens', an anonymous contributor to The Gamekeeper and Countryside Magazine *of 1940, experienced that familiar conversion from poacher to gamekeeper; here he writes of the habits of hares, and describes a cunning way to deter the hare netters:*

'In March when hares are pairing, four or five may frequently be found together in one field. Although wild they seem to lose much of their natural timidity and during this month I usually reaped a rich harvest. I was always careful to set my wires and snares on the side <u>opposite</u> to that from which the game would come, for this reason – that hares approach any place through which they are about to pass in a zig-zag manner. They come on, playing and frisking, stopping now and then to nibble the herbage. Then they canter, making wide leaps at right angles to their path and sit listening upon their haunches. A freshly impressed footmark turns them back. Of course these traces are certain to be left if the snare be set on the <u>near</u> side of the gate or fence and then a hare will refuse to take it, even when hard pressed.

'Now here is a wrinkle to any keeper who would care to accept it. Where poaching is prevalent and hares abundant, <u>every hare on the estate should be netted</u>, for it is a fact well known to every poacher versed in his craft that an escaped hare that has once been netted can never be retaken. The process, however, will effectually frighten a small percentage of hares off the land altogether.'

· UP AGAINST THE PROFESSIONALS ·

'Tower Bird', Tim Sedgewick of Shooting Times *fame, writing in the magazine in 1957 describes an encounter with longdog men, a rural curse then in its infancy but now rife across much of the British countryside, especially in the eastern counties where hares still abound. Then, as now, the fines imposed by the courts were laughable:*

'One afternoon a few years before the recent war, two of us were feeding pheasants in a covert on the high downs when we spied a car pull up in front of a half built bungalow along a track leading from a nearby village. Out of the car climbed four men and four "long dogs", the men shutting these in the bungalow before two of them advanced boldly to a hollow in the land well within the limits of our ground.

'Quickly completing our job we managed to approach within several hundred yards of the hollow without being seen, where we took up position to await events. As the light weakened the men emerged from their hiding place and began setting snares in a line along the many hare runs plainly visible from the slope. It would have been a simple enough matter to have walked out and accosted them, but the keeper knows his job and it was not our object to accuse them of poaching by day but by night.

'Anxiously we watched them working further and further from us while the hands of our watches crept all too slowly forward. At length, greatly disappointed, we were forced to take action ere we lost sight of the men behind a shoulder in the downs. We knew well enough what their game was – to set up a long line of snares and then to drive a wide expanse of downs with the aid of the dogs, towards the line.

'When we came up to the men, recognition was mutual. They belonged to a gang of professional poachers living in the suburbs of a town ten miles away. Knowing too something of their records we expected an assault but for some reason this did not mature. We picked up some forty snares, relieved them of thirty more and walked down the track to take the number of their car. In due course the case came to court where the defendents were fined £2 each and they muttered threats to us as they left the building. One of these men had over forty previous convictions for poaching against him, the other over thirty, including assaults on gamekeepers and police. In spite of the fact that they had arrived in a nearly new car they were given a week or a fortnight to pay the fines.

'A few months later the same two men were caught nearby on his ground by a single handed keeper who wears glasses. One man showing fight, the keeper, knowing him to be a pugilist and a dangerous character, drew a heavy ash stick across his face, re-breaking his nose, and instantly took after the second whom he caught. On this occasion the penalties inflicted were greater because of the assault.'

· HARE-CHASING BY LAND ROVER ·

Chippy Smith, the old-time, part-time keeper from Devon, finds as others have done before him, that chasing game from a moving vehicle at night with a loaded gun on board can be a hair- (or in this case 'hare'-) raising experience. He was lucky to come out uninjured, although more than half a century has served to soften the memory.

'It was snowing so heavily that all work on the construction of the runway ceased. My mate and I had the use of a Land Rover and all we lacked was a gun to bag a few rabbits and the odd hare. In the end we borrowed an old hammer double-barrelled 12-bore from the foreman on the site.

'Travelling up the taxi-ing track we had not gone very far before we spotted two hares in the headlights. I was perched on the bonnet with a headlight between my legs. I pointed out the hares to my mate who was doing the driving. He put his foot down to the floor chasing after the hare but seemed to have forgotten me clinging on for dear life.

'Unknown to him we were getting dangerously close to a half-filled drainage trench: I knew well where it was, for that was my job, drains and outfalls. I began to hammer on the windscreen shouting at him to slow down.

'All of a sudden he hit the earth spoil thick with snow. The Land Rover dug in and I went flying. When I hit the ground the gun went off, but no damage as the snow was pretty deep by this time.

'When I walked slowly back he said, "Did you get it?"

'I said, "No! You didn't throw me far enough!"

'Happy Days!'

· COLOURED RABBITS ·

The keepers use an old trick to check whether their rabbits are being poached but the poachers are wise to it. This anonymous account comes from 1880.

'On the confines of a large estate a rather clever trick was once played on us. Each year about half a dozen black or white rabbits were turned down in certain woods. Whilst feeding, these stood out conspicuously from the rest and were religiously preserved. Upon these the keepers kept a close watch and when any were missing it was suspected what was going on and the watching strength was increased.

'As soon as we detected the trick, we were careful to let the coloured rabbits go free. We found that it was altogether to our interest to preserve them.'

One imagines that this trick, though ingenious, had a limited life span. Given the notoriously promiscuous habits of rabbits it would not be long before half the rabbits in the warren would be coloured oddly.

· RABBITY DICK'S BAD LUCK ·

A charming minor work on poaching is the little book Pennine Poacher *written in 1982 by and about Richard Fawcett, better known as 'Rabbity Dick' and whom we have already met (p28), recounting some of his own exploits. He was mainly a rabbit man, but in his time he took a few pheasants and walked the moors for grouse. Working in the pre-myxamotosis days before and during the last war, his book is a fascinating reminiscence of those hard times in the Yorkshire Dales. 'Rabbity Dick' worked all his life on the railway often in a signal box. Taking game was a way of life to most of the rural railwaymen then, for they chugged gently past fields full of feeding game and it was an easy matter to set a wire.*

In this extract Dick has had bad luck twice running and loses not only his new net but what might otherwise have been the all time record bag of rabbits from the Bolton Abbey area.

'I admit now that I turned into a right villain of a poacher, no words can describe how wicked, but how I enjoyed it. I needed more and more rabbits to satisfy my friends, so I bought two new long nets — one 50 yards and one 100 yards in length. I started going out netting after 10 o'clock on several nights in the week if the weather was right. There were so many rabbits so near that I could go out and get maybe fifteen or twenty and be back home within the hour. I won't mention the times I have come back with nothing.

'A few hundred yards up the road from Bolton Abbey station is a row of houses known as Hambleton Cottages. In the first house near the road lived the retired head keeper of the Devonshire Estate and his three sons. Another retired man lived on the same row. On Summer evenings they used to sit out at the back of the cottages and try and count the rabbits sat out in the small meadow on the other side of the road, perhaps seventy yards away, nearer Skipton. They would get in the region of 600 each count. Disturb them and they would rush into the plantation like a cloud. I had my eye on them; I had previously been able to stride it out and found the 100 yard net would be just right.

'With long netting one must get going early in the Autumn when the bulk of the rabbits are still around. When it gets into November and towards Christmas I would still get a few but by then the rabbit catchers had been round and lessened them considerably. When I netted them in late September on a stormy Sunday night I had so many rabbits in the net the weight of them broke the top and bottom cord and they all escaped except seven. I knew I had spoiled them, I would never get the same again. I am sure I had all six hundred in first time.

'I waited for a few weeks until the rabbits had got over their fright and their nerves had steadied up then had another go. As always I had waited for a black wild night when the tree tops were whipping each other. I set my net quickly, crept across the road and into the field opposite, creeping along under the wall until I was opposite my field. I would then cross the road and go over the wall and away; I was behind them now. I was dressed as usual for my job in some running shorts and pumps – and could I run! I had always a light stick to switch about with and sometimes tap against my legs to keep the rabbits running.

'I had made a bad slip up this time also. I had not noticed that there were now some sheep in the field; I should have checked that earlier. They saw me coming, snorted and ran away, right into the net, carrying it along for some yards which resulted in a struggling mass of sheep and one or two rabbits squealing like heck. All this was happening perhaps only forty yards from the roadway, each car coming from Skipton shining its lights momentarily as it passed by, over the very part of the field in which I was having my exercise. And only one hundred yards down the road lived the retired head keeper and his son Adrian who was now also a gamekeeper.

I always carried a sharp knife for legging and gutting the rabbits and eventually I got the sheep free, though some did break loose. Thankfully they were not horned sheep. The net was ruined, and how many rabbits were mixed with the sheep I do not remember.'

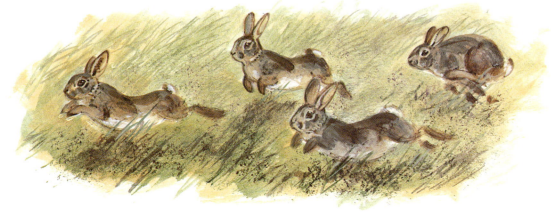

· A BRAWL WITH GYPSIES ·

One of the latest and best autobiographical books on poaching is The Great Game *by Harold Wyman. This Welsh poacher, the genuine article, describes his life and times and tells of some hair-raising adventures in his long poaching life. He was a rabbit specialist but also knew a thing or two about pheasants and salmon. In this extract he has a little trouble in the pub and shows scant respect for the gentler sex; but then, those were rough times . . .*

'. . . Spring [his lurcher] became a legend among the coursing fraternity in and around Wrexham and in all the years I saw him course hares in the company of other dogs, I never saw another dog outstay him. In fact, I never saw another dog stay with him to the end of a long hard course.

'Spring sired a very good bitch out of the blue bitch. My mate Patsy Burk owned her, she could not jump like her sire but could stay well and accounted for many a hare.

'In the days when I enjoyed hare coursing, I never did seek the death of the creature. I enjoyed the thrill of the chase, but was quite pleased when, after a great test of wits and stamina, the hare came out with colours flying.

'The discussion of lurcher capabilities reminds me of a brawl with gypsies. Many years

ago a friend, Patsy Burke and I were conversing over a pint of ale in a public house situated in the town centre and named the Feathers Inn. Patsy was a very dear friend of long standing and is now, I am sorry to say, dead and gone with so many of my friends. Though he enjoyed night poaching his great passion was hare coursing. At five foot nine, slim built with hair of ginger hue that was common with Irish ancestors, Patsy was deceptive but he was a useful man to have protecting one's back in the event of a brawl.

'Pat and I were enjoying our conversation when a fair number of people entered the bar room. We were aware from their mode of dress and speech that they were members of the gypsy fraternity and Pat informed me that they were not the usual trouble-making kind. This information seemed a little odd to me as I had learned from past experience that most gypsies or tinkers were reasonable within limits when sober, but once the local brew had been sampled their whole attitude changed towards the local people. This occasion turned out to be no exception.

'Patsy entered into conversation with one of them and inevitably the subject of lurchers came up. Now most lurcher men will tell you, just mention hare coursing among the gypsy fraternity and one of them always has a lurcher back at the caravan which can kill five out of five hares any morning. The person Patsy was discussing coursing with was a large, overweight man with the typical black greasy hair and dark skin of the gypsy. "All right, my brother," he said to Patsy. "Sunday morning for a bet of two pounds a side." There had been a challenge and I knew Patsy was going to run Spring so I also offered to bet a couple of pounds but the offer was declined with a particularly insulting remark. I immediately came back at him with "I have never seen a hedge crawler's lurcher get more than three hundred yards. All gypsy dogs," I said, "are fed on bread and Oxo." As I have said, the gypsy was a big heavy man, but when he moved it was with surprising agility. Pat was brushed aside and the lapels of my jacket were in his powerful grip.

'I moved quickly first one way then in the opposite direction, his balance was broken and he was thrown by a judo move which in English we call an "Inner Reeper". I promptly fell on top of him and heard one of the gypsy women call out "get the dingle mush off". I found that this translated means "get the mad one off". Moments after I heard this I received a severe blow to the side of my head so I put the fat man out of the game and got to my feet to face the person who had delivered the blow.

'It was a large-boned gypsy woman with a bottle of brown ale in her hand and she was about to line me up for a repeat dose of the medicine. I was left with no alternative but to flatten her which caused no pricks of conscience at the time or subsequently. Anyway, Pat, myself and a couple were battling away for dear life when the police arrived and order was restored . . .'

· COUNTER MEASURES ·

'Rabbity Dick' strikes up a friendship with the mole catcher known to history as 'Mowdie Bill'. Bill had been catching rabbits in Swaledale but suspected that the farmer had been taking rabbits from his snares and keeping them in the barn. He had marked some rabbits by nicking their ears so he could be positive of the thefts. He recruits Dick to help him get them back – with interest. They choose a Wednesday night for the raid because at 9.00pm everyone listened to the News on the wireless and after that it was boxing, so every farmer in the dale would be glued to his set. This tale is also from Richard Fawcett's Pennine Poacher.

'Bill had a big new motorcycle. We left Apperset at about 7.30, me on the pillion, well wrapped up with a couple of cowbands each to thread the rabbits on. Up through Simonstone and on to Stagsfell fell and Buttertubs Pass, a bit cold over the top. How that big bike roared over the mountain road, fairly sucking in the frosty air. We freewheeled down into the valley as far as Thwaite, then went up the dale at reduced speed, trying to make as little noise as possible for it was a bad night for the job – too quiet, with no wind, no moon but a very starry sky. Swaledale is still a fairly quiet valley but nothing compared with those days. Electricity had not arrived then.

'Somewhere past Keld, Bill stopped the bike and I helped him push it through a field gate nearly fifty yards along the wall side. He said, "Never leave your tackle too near a gate, someone might see it too easily. That's the place!" I could see the lights of the farm nearly quarter of a mile up the hillside on the other side of the River Swale.

'Apparently he did not want me to go to the farm with him for he said, "You stay here by the bike". He looked at his watch, "About ten to nine," he said. I waited there patiently and uneasily. I could hear owls hooting up and down the dale – they always hoot more on frosty nights. A few seconds after 9 o'clock I heard a dog at the farm start barking, then shut up sharply with a yelp. I guessed what had happened, Bill's boot. Perhaps twenty five minutes after leaving me Bill arrived back quietly with a tremendous bundle of rabbits. He was panting hard, for the last fifty yards at my side of the river along which he had just come were quite steep, and he was wet with sweat. He dropped the rabbits and his jacket saying, "The buggers! My marked rabbits are amongst them. There are a lot left in the shed and I am going back for some more." He was gone again. I tidied what he had dropped into two even bundles for easy carrying. Each was almost enough for one man to carry.

'He was soon back. Even without a jacket he was sweating heavily and almost out of puff, with nearly as many

RABBIT RAIDERS

rabbits as the first time. We evened them out into four bundles, carried them to the top of the hill, then wheeled the bike to the hilltop, laid a big bundle of rabbits on the tank across his knees and hung some round his neck and down at the front side. I loaded up on the pillion with a huge bundle on each shoulder then we let the bike run off down the hill in gear. We crept down the hill as far as Thwaite, then turned right for the big climb to the Buttertubs and on to the top.

RABBIT RAIDERS

'I could tell my pilot was having difficulty controlling the bike with all that weight and it was much worse going up hill because it took all the weight off the front wheel and the lights were shining up into the sky. The bike did roar coming over early in the evening, but it roared harder coming up that hill in low gear on the way back. If anyone had been standing outside enjoying the night as far down as Reeth or as far up as Dale Head, they would surely have heard us.

'Over the top we had to stop several times on account of rabbit heads getting into the spokes of the wheels but we reached home without accident. It was no trouble to the motor bike but how the back tyre stood it is a marvel. When we got back to Apperset we counted the rabbits and we had more than a hundred. Such was his revenge for those people stealing his. He gave me £1 which was a half a week's wage then. I was well satisfied.

'Bill told me later that the dog jumped out at him suddenly and he gave it one just as sudden. When he went back the second time he could hear the commentator shouting, "A left to the jaw . . . a right to the chin . . ." so he loaded up again.'

. . . many lords of manors who would rather lose an ounce of their own blood than a brace of their pheasants, have striven to preserve every head of game by day while the poachers, unmolested, were clearing it wholesale during the night. Sometimes the manors were invaded even by day by old stagers from a garrison who select market days when the tenants are absent and windy weather when they can manoeuvre to leeward and outflank the keepers.

. . . gentlemen poachers have, by running away through pretended fear, drawn a gamekeeper off his boundary. Some with a polite bow and shrug of the shoulders have pretended to be foreigners who do not understand a syllable of English. Others, regardless of either word or credit, most faithfully assure the keepers that they have got leave from the master, inquire after his health and pretend to be on the most intimate acquaintance with him.

. . . Some attempt to carry their point by sheer bullying; threatening to box with or shoot the keepers and talk of 'satisfaction' – 'pistols', 'fighting in the saw pit' – and hold forth vaunting proposals in which, if they were once taken at their word, they would be the very first to sport the white feather. They are not all men of war who strut about with colossal brass spurs and ten shillings worth of hair like a magpies nest, pasted round their jowls.

From *Instructions to Young Sportsmen*,
Lt Col Peter Hawker, 1833

WAGGONLOAD OF MONKEYS

· THE WAYS OF THE POACHER ·

The ways of the poacher were well known: Stonehenge in 1856 gives a checklist of some of their more evil practices, including the fact that a simple shepherd's smock could conceal both a poacher and his booty beneath its folds.

'There are two classes of poachers, the day and the night poacher. The day poacher is usually solitary, night poachers on the contrary are gregarious. The solitary poacher in most instances displays more strategem than those who go out in murderous gangs, clearing everything before them and braving with a bold and determined front, every danger.

'The solitary poacher for instance, perceives that a long drain or small rivulet runs in a certain direction separating field from field. The communication by highway is across a bridge and the hares during their time of feeding, can only cross from one part to the other by means of that bridge. Therefore the poacher sets his net across that bridge and waits in ambush. In the course of a short time probably a hare or two are caught in the net when he is immediately at hand to secure them.

'The same trick is resorted to at a gate which leads into cover in an open field. The gate is thrown open and the net fixed between the posts. [This is *not* how it was done; the gate was left shut and the net draped from its top: JH.] A lurcher scours the field, the hares make for the wood immediately and are entangled and thus secured. The same plan will likewise apply to rabbits just at nightfall or rather later.

'To these tricks may be added the fact that the gun of the poacher is made to unscrew so that he can put the breech in one pocket and secrete the barrel on the other side of his jacket. The latter part of the gun can also be used in case of danger as a very formidable weapon of attack or defence.

'The poacher beside him keeps two or three dogs of lurcher breed which answers his purpose best as they hunt without giving mouth, possess a good nose and are very sagacious animals. These dogs are kept in dark cellars and are only taken out during the night so that in fact, they scarcely ever see the daylight.

'Nevertheless, they are as eager for the sport as their masters themselves for whom they do good service in the destruction of game.

'In day poaching, a wet afternoon, a Sunday morning or a market day are selected, when the farmers are neither at home nor in the fields. Snares and nets are then set in every direction in the very heart of the preserves. A lurcher dog properly trained for the purpose that never

barks, is then cast off by a motion
of the hand to rouse the game which
is soon caught and stowed away in sacks in some
secret place until the darkness of night prevails
when it is cautiously fetched away.

'If the poacher is detected in the cover he motions his
dog to leave the spot which it instantly obeys. He has nothing
on him, he is not armed and he has a thousand excuses to make, that he has lost his way,
or is seeking for lost cattle, and is probably suffered to depart. Sometimes he is not allowed
to leave without a search, for even under the simple garb of a shepherd the poacher
endeavours to conceal his real character *and his booty!*

'Occasionally a gang of night poachers divide themselves into two parties, one of which
will proceed to the outside of the woods near a high road and there commence firing their
guns or pistols in order to draw the attention of the watchers to that point, whilst the
other is effecting as much destruction as possible in another part of the preserve. When
the former perceive their opponents in the direction where they first commenced firing,
they immediately retreat for the purpose of drawing them away from the best preserves
and afterwards make their escape either by the turnpike road or into another liberty.

'Thus they leave their companions to pursue their system of destruction in perfect
safety or to make good their retreat. All share equally in the plunder.'

· THE SQUIRE'S GUEST ·

A Victorian rascal shows inventiveness and cheek in this escapade, taking advantage of a squire absent from his estate for a few days together with a keeper new to the locality. It was not unknown for guests of the squire to come down and shoot his land in an informal manner, and the keeper would be expected to attend them. This is more of a youthful escapade than a serious poaching venture, our hero dresses up as a gentleman and arrives at the great estate:

'Well, I had arranged with a confederate to act as bag carrier. He was to be very servile and not forget to touch his cap at pretty frequent intervals. After "making-up" as a country squire (I had closely studied that species on The Bench), and providing a luncheon in keeping with my temporary squiredom, we started for the woods.

'It was a bright morning in the last week of October and game, hares, pheasants and woodcock was exceedingly plentiful. The first firing brought up the keeper who touched his hat in a most respectful fashion. He behaved in short, precisely as I would have had him behave. I lost no time in quietly congratulating him on the number and quality of his birds, told him that his master would return from town tomorrow (which I had learned incidentally), and ended by handing him my cartridge bag to carry. A splendid bag of birds had been made by luncheon time and the viands which constituted the meal were very much in keeping with my assumed position.

'Dusk came at the close of the short October afternoon, and with it the end of our day's sport. The bag was spread out in one of the rides in the wood and in imagination I can see it now, thirty-seven pheasants, nine hares, five woodcock, a few rabbits, some cushats and the usual "miscellaneous". The man of gaiters was dispatched a couple of miles for a cart to carry the spoil and a substantial tip gave speed to his not unwilling legs.

'The game, however, was not to occupy the cart. A donkey with panniers was waiting in a clump of brush by the covert side and as soon as the panniers were packed, its head was turned homeward over a bit of wild moorland. With the start obtained, chase would have been useless had it ever been contemplated – which it never was.

'I need not detail the sequel to the incident here and may say that it was somewhat painful to myself as well as my bag carrier. And I am sorry to say that the keeper was summarily dismissed by the enraged squire as a reward for his innocence. As to the coverts, they were so well stocked that after a few days' rest there appeared as much as ever and the contents of our little bag were hardly missed.'

· A CAUTION FOR OLD BUGG ·

Dick Townsend is a retired Norfolk keeper, who over the years has sent me many fine tales and reminiscences. Here he tells the tale of the undoing of 'Old Bugg', the rabbit snarer:

'This is the name he was known as by the people in the village but we keepers lengthened his nick-name by two letters; we had good cause. It wasn't that he was a gun man and he didn't worry us unduly by being after our birds. His love was snaring rabbits and this we did not mind and even gave him permission to snare in some of the Park and the odd field where we thought he would not be doing us any harm. However, he would not stop at this and every so often he would wander where we did not want him.

'The real reason he was unwelcome was that we did a lot of long netting with 300 yards of net and wanted to keep our best places from being disturbed. You don't get many really good nights for netting in the season and normally a good night to go is often a good night for snaring too. There were two lodges separated by a wood on either side that led to the Park road and Old Bugg lived in one of them. When coming from the Park you had to go through the wood which was about 200 yards wide and ran each side of the lodges for a quarter of a mile.

'One November afternoon I was cycling through the Park towards Bugg's house and there was a very thick fog; you could see no further than 30 or 40 yards ahead. I was nearly up to where the road went through the wood, and glancing to my right where there was a wire fence coming from the wood I was just able to see though the fog a form bending down on the other side.

'I guessed straight away that it was the old Bugger snaring again and he knew well he had no right to be snaring there as it was one of our best spots for netting. I knew he thought he could get away with it in the fog. However, I had other ideas for I was almost certain that after he had set his snares he would be at the end of the wood where a lane came from Park Farm and back the other side of the wood to his house.

'I kept a safe distance and as fast as he set them I took them up and as sure as Hell, after he had set the last one he made his way to the lane. I quickly pulled up the last one as I knew I could be back to his house before him and needless to say I was, and after hanging his snares on his gate I went to tell the head keeper what I had done.

'He had a really good laugh and said, "I can picture his face when he opens the gate and finds the snares at home before him". Then he went on to say, "It's no good; he doesn't take any notice of us telling him where he can and cannot go but perhaps this will put him off a little." However, I can tell you it didn't and his next stepping out of line happened on one of our shooting days.

'We used to shoot three days running every fortnight and on our last day we were shooting on the keeper's beat which was the furthest away from Bugg's home. At lunch time the game cart went to the game larder to unload and when it returned at about 2.45 I walked over with some

more birds when the driver said he had just seen old Bugg setting his snares. "Which field was he in?" I asked. "He was setting them in Warren field", was his reply.

'He really had done it this time for no way would we have him there; we had been fair to him but he must be taught a lesson. The Head Keeper and I had already planned what we would do if we caught him breaking the rules again and this was a great opportunity for me to carry out the plan. There was only one more drive so I asked Clark quietly if it was all right if I went off then as the old Bugger had been seen "at it" in the Warren field. He knew exactly what I meant and said, "By all means; get going and make sure he doesn't see you."

'I went straight to the game cart and picked out a bird that wasn't badly shot. This was easily done as it is our usual practice that if a bird was caught by one of the dogs or a beater, one of its toes would be cut off to let us know there was no shot in it. This done, I set off making my way to Warren field. I got there just in time to see Bugg walking to his cycle which stood against the hedge just inside the gate. Now I had to make sure he was well out of the way before I made a move but when he got to his bike he did not seem in any hurry. He just stood and kept looking round, then decided to fill his pipe and light it. I was beginning to get a little worried as the light was fading, but then it came to me that no doubt he was having a good look to make sure that nobody was pulling up his snares behind him! Anyway, a few minutes later he was on his bike and well away.

'Now I had to set to work to find a suitable snare to put the pheasant in and also a convenient place I could hide in the morning when he came to look at them. At the same time I knew it had to be one of the first snares he set in the afternoon that had the pheasant in it, for most of the birds would be in the wood waiting to go up to perch when the later ones were set. Also, it could not have got in the snare in the morning or it would have been still warm on his arrival.

'I had to make a bit of a show where the bird had struggled to get out, but in my favour there was a little light rain starting which would cover all tracks by the morning. I have pointed out these details because anyone who had done as much snaring as Bugg knew all the ins and outs of the trade.

'Now, to put your minds at rest whoever may be reading this, the Head Keeper and I had no intention of prosecuting him for poaching or taking game; we just wanted to scare him enough to keep him off the ground he was not allowed to use.

'In the morning I was waiting and just as he was about to put the pheasant in his inside pocket after removing the snare I walked up and said, "What have you got there?" His reply was, "The bloody thing must have got in after I set it yesterday. I can assure you this don't happen ever; I'm not trying to snare your birds." I told him I would have to report him to the Head Keeper and he said, "No, no, don't do that; I don't want the old bird", and he threw it at me. I replied, "I'm afraid I'll have to; you are snaring in the worst place you could be; he'll be coming up to see you." He remarked that nothing seemed to be going right lately, but did not mention finding his snares on his garden gate.

'In the meantime we had told the policeman exactly what we had done and asked if, in a couple of days he would call round and take a dummy statement from Bugg. Being a good friend of ours he agreed and added that he would tell him he would hear when the case was due to come up. We knew this would not be Bugg's biggest worry though, for in those times anyone found poaching on the estate who lived in one of the houses was given two month's notice to quit and after having lived there most of his life, Bugg was a worried man.

'Six months afterwards in May 1938 we had taken our rearing hut and coops onto that very field where I had pulled up his snares in the fog. He came to me in the rearing field and said. "Have you heard when they're going to bring up my case?" "Well," I told him. "it may not be until you are seen snaring again on the fields where you have been told to keep off." His old face lit up, and as he turned to go he said, "Thanks for bringing the snares home; you are good old boys."

'I was only there another two years as I went into the RAF after the war started, but Clark the Head Keeper was there for another 25 years and told me there was never any more trouble from old Bugg, right until he died.

* * *

'At this point I would like to put down my views about rabbit poachers which were the same as my old Head Keeper's used to be. I would never prosecute a man who was definitely only after a rabbit providing he was not using a gun or long netting at night, trying to bolt rabbits at night using lurchers or any other dog day or night and providing the snares were all set on the flat, not in ditches, hedges or long grass, furrows, wire fences, bushes or any rough places.

'I have always said that if I'm not man enough to catch the real game poacher I would never try to make up for it by prosecuting the poor fellow trying to get a brace of rabbits for his family dinner. In my fifty-one years as a gamekeeper I have never taken a person to court for catching a rabbit. I have taken at least twenty-five game-poaching cases at night as well as day and enjoyed every minute of it.

'This is not to say that some of them I've caught rabbiting were not put off the ground pretty quickly, but lots of others became good friends and I let them go on certain places. In return I got a great deal of help at times and also some very useful information.'

· THE SALMON POACHERS ·

Thomas Todd is a north country poacher, one of whose favourite pursuits was salmon poaching. Here he describes a narrow escape when his quick-wittedness saved him a beating and worse: this extract was written in 1932.

'We had joined the beck where it meets the Tees and were making our way steadily upwards. Naturally we knew our business well and had already made a fair haul of salmon when we became alarmed.

'When fleetness of foot is necessary to make a getaway from watcher chaps, fish already caught are a hindrance. As we laid and listened we were lucky enough to catch a sight of the metal facings and helmets of the police who were accompanied by keepers. They had seen our light from a distance and were making a beeline for it and were trusting that we would have no idea of their whereabouts and that they would be able to drop on top of us before we could make an escape.

'Our difficulty was that we could not unload our catch and dash for it without betraying that we were a very few yards from where they had struck the river. Our lantern had been dashed at the onset. We lay in the bushes and felt the thudding of our hearts.

'I had made up my mind that I was not going to leave the fish I carried because it was a case of "no fish, no beer", nor was I prepared to dump it for them to find and lay watch for us returning for it. If we were caught we would be badly mauled. If the worst happened we were armed with a couple of cobbles apiece with which we hoped to flatten at least four of them.

'There was no time to lose before the police and watchers would divide and search the bank up and down and they would be bound to find us. Above us was a pool which was well known; my companion read my mind and whispered, "How-way, an' mek nee noise". At the foot of the pool I had in mind is a bend where more salmon have been poached than ever took a hook. The watchers would know of it also. No time must be lost in getting there. As swiftly as we could and testing each footing lest we disturb a loose stone, we made progress as best we might. Quickly and under cover of my coat I relit the lantern and hung it close to the water on a bush so that it could easily be seen at a distance by our pursuers.

'It turned out as I bargained. By the time they had stolen up to the lantern and surrounded it in the full expectation of catching us red-handed, we were well on our way back to Middleton.'

· TRICKS OF THE TRADE ·

John Watson's Victorian account of poaching tricks mentions the old dodge of burning sulphur under the beak of a roosting bird until, stupefied by the fumes, it falls to the ground. To my knowledge this trick has never been performed save in story books and is part of the poacher's store of mythology. Our pheasants certainly would not sit while 'a bunch of matches…is lighted and held under the boughs on which [they] are perched'. The idea of a firefly as a foresight for a dark night is, however, a novel one though equally unlikely; and the writer clearly has no first-hand knowledge of trail-netting.

'In securing a booty of pheasants, a moonlight night is fixed upon. Air guns are often used, some of which will kill at a distance of thirty yards. The poacher is well acquainted with the spots where the pheasants roost and on a clear night they can be distinctly seen perched on the boughs and are easily shot. If from the nature of the preserve there should be some difficulty in getting a clear shot a differing plan is pursued.

'Major Bevan in his work *Thirty Years in India* whilst alluding to the subject of night shooting says, "I tried the experiment of fastening a firefly on the sight of my gun and found it is the greatest value in directing the eye along the barrel and enabling me to cover my object distinctly." The aim of the poacher is sometimes directed by a different light. He perhaps can see the pheasant but not distinctly and should the moon have gone down, contrives to place himself in such a direction that he can have a bright star in the line of the bird.

'He bends down until he has got the star in position, just over the bird for instance, he takes his aim by the star and kills it. Other means are also adopted in case of the danger arising from firearms. A bunch of matches placed at the end of a long stick, is lighted and held under the boughs on which the pheasants are perched. They become stifled and fall to the ground senseless when they are instantly secured and killed.

'Among the many tricks resorted to by the poacher for the purpose of deceiving the keeper, a favourite one is to place a dead hare in a snare near his house. The keeper soon discovers this and proceeds with an assistant to watch the hare, secreting himself at a short distance in expectation that the setter of the snare will come to the spot to fetch his victim. Whilst the deluded keeper is thus employed, the poachers are busily at work in another direction with their snares and whilst he is watching the dead hare, they are securing as many as they can conveniently carry home.

'Much practice enables the poacher to set his snares in an unerring manner and, in order that the wire may be as pliant as possible, the snares previous to being used are placed within a bundle of hay. The hay is set on fire and the embers are allowed to cool gradually before the snares are taken ot. By this process the wire is rendered so tough and flexible that it can be bent in any form to answer the purpose of the poacher.

'The snarer however, is liable to be thwarted in his designs in consequence of the hare's raising a loud cry of distress which may be heard at some distance. The poacher prevents this where the situation requires it, by bending down the branch of a large tree, a young oak or other sapling. To these the snares are attached and the branch of the young tree is pegged down into the ground. The snares are set in runs in the wood and when the hare is caught, her struggles detach the peg, up springs the tree and poor puss is hung aloft and, of course, can make no noise.

'Great destruction is also effected by the drag partridge net for, by its skilful application all the coveys on the estate may be secured in the course of a few nights. This engine, if engine it may be called, is about forty yards in length and twenty five in width. It is composed of silk and hair twisted together with meshes at proper distance. It is rather an expensive article but is very strong and when folded up can be contained in a moderate sized pocket which is a matter of great convenience.

'Through the meshes on one side of this net a long stout cord is passed, considerably longer indeed than the net itself. On the other side a number of weights are attached for the purpose of keeping it down when it is dragged by two men who each have hold of one end of the long cord. They know well enough where the coveys assemble at night.

'If after proceeding to the locality they find that one covey is close at hand and the others are not a long way off, they use a "call", a close imitation of the cry of the male bird. By exercising a little dexterity in this respect, three or four coveys can be decoyed into one field.

'When this necessary preliminary is accomplished, then commences the work of destruction. The net is spread out a short distance from an adjacent hedge. Each man takes hold of his own end of the cord and the weighted net is dragged over the field. The first attempt may be a failure so the next breadth is tried. It proves successful. The net is drawn over perhaps the whole of two coveys of birds which immediately begin to flutter.

'Each man then lets the net fall to the ground and commences to walk along the cord til the spot is reached where the partridges are caught. They are then killed and bagged. There is no noise, no report of a gun as in the case of killing pheasants. On the least approach of danger the net is pocketed and the poachers make the best of their way to the nearest high road or take a route so circuitous as to elude all detection and arrive home before daybreak.'

· A WOMAN'S MISTAKE ·

Poachers disguising themselves as women was an old trick, and an old trick is always worth trying, especially in the days when those voluminous skirts could conceal many a brace of illicit birds. Jacko was a clever poacher, never taking many pheasants and for long evading suspicion, but he made one fatal mistake when dressed as a woman on one of his raids, by not getting sufficiently 'into character'. Dick Townsend, the retired Norfolk keeper who sent me so many tales, tells this true story from his old Norfolk days.

'I always thought that Jacko, who lived in the next village, was the most unfortunate poacher to be caught, for he had really got the job sorted out over the previous four or five seasons.

'Jacko was a very likeable fellow, quiet, a good mixer, never caused any trouble and the last person you would ever suspect of poaching. I must point out that he was not an "all night" man out to get a big bag, just two or three birds and then on his bike and off home.

'He would go about three times every month when the moon and the weather were right, and the few shillings he earned were helpful but not half as rewarding as the thrill he got from the job. Many were the times when the police and keepers had said "Goodnight" to him when they were out looking for poachers and he was on his way home with two or three birds. The one thing he had to avoid, as you will see, was engaging in long conversations. This is how he managed to operate so successfully until that fatal night.

'He kept a woman's cycle in his shed, the old upright type with a carrier on the back where he strapped a small suitcase to carry his folding 4.10, sawn off to fit, and also to bring home any birds he might get. Then he dressed himself up like a woman, with a long black dress and a mac and a wide-brimmed hat.

'Jacko lived in an isolated house down a lane so there was no worry about being seen going to and from his home. He would often shoot a brace of birds which were roosting near the roadside knowing full well he would be back on his bike and the birds in his case by the time anyone came and even if they did, which happened more than once, no one was going to challenge or suspect a woman cycling home at night.

'Well, all this came to a sad end for Jacko. He had been out on one of his poaching larks and was on his way home. As he came through the Park he had to open the gate, which was closed to keep the cattle in, and after closing it to make sure that no one was about he decided to "answer a call of Nature" before continuing his three-mile journey home.

'This is where he made his fatal mistake, for he stood up when he should have crouched down! He set off home thinking that all was well, but unbeknown to him he had been seen by a courting couple who had hidden when they saw him coming on his cycle. The girl was a maid from the Hall who had sneaked out to see her boyfriend without anyone knowing, so didn't want to be seen. The couple were speechless, couldn't believe their eyes and ended up having a good laugh.

'But the girl was related to one of the keepers so she asked her boyfriend to call and see him on his way home and explain exactly what they had seen, and to relate that this "woman" was definitely a man! They were not to know, of course, that this person had been poaching, but they knew there was something fishy in it somewhere.

'Poor Jacko was caught within the week, for every policeman and keeper around were on the lookout for the woman cycling home at night with a suitcase strapped to her carrier. Even so, it was not a good cop when they got him.

'The Police wanted to get in first so they stopped him on his way out and when they searched him there was no game in the case, only the gun and a few feathers and some blood. The keepers were not very pleased about this as they had arranged to make sure he was challenged only after being followed and watched until they were certain that he had some birds in his possession.

'Jacko was fined only £2, so I suppose that in the end he had a lucky escape.'

· TRAIL-NETTERS OUTWITTED ·

Dick Townsend kindly supplied me with this account of how he once employed one of the oldest tricks in the book to thwart a gang of trail-netters:

'My girlfriend and I had been to a dance, and after cycling home with her I started on my seven-mile journey home. This was in 1940 during the war so all lights on vehicles had to be cut to a minimum which meant only a half-inch slit for the light to come through on cycle lamps.

'It was a pretty dark night and I had gone about a mile and a half and was going up a hill – needless to say not very quickly – when a bird flew close over me coming from the field on my left. I couldn't be sure what kind of bird it was but I knew from experience it was not a bird which normally flew at night; it was one which had been disturbed.

'I stopped and put my light off, not that it could be seen from the fields as there was a fairly high grass bank each side of the road. I rested my foot on the bank and listened for a while. I heard a slight noise which I was unable to identify, that is until it got nearer. Then there was no mistaking what was happening: the stubble was being netted.

'Now, what was I to do? I had got my best clothes on and I wasn't sure how many of them there were on the job and I did not really want to get knocked about when it was nothing to do with me. However, I could not ignore the challenge and suddenly an old idea came into my head which I hoped would work.

'I could hear the rustle of the net on the stubble getting closer but still could not pick out their forms. I hoped they would be about 40 or 50 yards away when I made my move for if I could see them, they could see me, and that was the last thing I wanted to happen. I thought, "Now's the time!" – I dared not chance letting them get any closer.

'I called out, not so loudly, but loud enough for them to know I was there and would hear. "Come on George! They're here. Get over to the right, Billy and we've got 'em!" No sooner had I said it than I knew my luck was in for I could hear them going helter skelter down the field.

'Then I walked in the direction they had run and you can imagine I was not long finding the net with my pointed-toed shoes which were very fashionable in those days. I soon gathered it up and was on my way home.

'About a week after there was a tale going round in my girlfriend's village that the keepers from Haveringland and Swannington chased some poachers netting but were not fast enough to catch them. That's how tales get about!'

· A RUSE WITH A MUSKET ·

Col George Hanger, that rumbustious old sportsman, describes in the extract below a simple trick played as often by keepers and poachers as by landowners, and one by which he cleared his wood permanently of a poaching gang. The same trick would not be acceptable today, as to which many keepers might say, more's the pity. This extract comes from Col Hanger's book To All Sportsmen *of 1814:*

'A most intimate and old friend of mine and an old soldier had a wood full of game close to his house, within at least a hundred and fifty yards. He had a large balcony up one pair of stairs which overlooked this wood. One night he heard some shots fired in this wood. He and his servant got up directly and planted themselves on the balcony. He always kept a soldier's musket for himself and one for his man with sixty rounds of ball cartridges for each.

'They fired each of them about twenty rounds at the very spots where they heard the guns go off, hollering out each time after they had fired, "For God's sake, take care of my spring guns!"

'Those gentlemen night sportsmen never came into his wood again.'

· THE POACHER'S LOOKOUT ·

The lookout or spy was an under-stated, shadowy member of the poaching team whose job was to spy out the ground while not arousing the suspicion of the keepers; on the contrary, he was the picture of innocence. Charles St John, who did his shooting at the height of the Victorian era, here gives a delightful thumbnail sketch of this shady individual, dressed, I am sad to note, 'more like a schoolmaster than a poacher' who was up to no good. This comes from his classic book A Tour of Sutherland.

'After having made their evening meal on the stubbles, which they always do in the Autumn and Winter between the hours of three and five, the old birds call their broods and collect them together. They then fly off to some grass field or other very bare ground, and having run about apparently in play for a little while, as soon as the light begins to fail, they fly off to some favourite spot in the field and huddling up together in a furrow, take up quarters for the night.

'Unluckily all this is done with a great deal of noise, the birds constantly calling to and answering each other and running to and fro with their heads conspicuously erect, thus plainly showing the netting poacher, who is sure to be on the lookout, where he may expect the best luck during the night.

'While this work is being carried on, you may see some fellow often dressed more like a schoolmaster than a poacher lounging listlessly about the lanes, leaning on the gates and smoking his pipe. You never suspect any sporting propensities can be concealed under the high-crowned beaver and swallow-tailed coat of this classical-looking gentleman who seems merely to be enjoying the beauty of the evening, although all the while he is watching with the eyes of a lynx the unsuspecting partridges as they run about calling to each other preparatory to going to roost.

'The fellow is thus able to form a pretty good guess as to where half a dozen coveys may be netted and he returns to his confederate, who in the meantime has been equally usefully employed at some alehouse or elsewhere in preparing and mending the nets.'

· CAUGHT BY A KEEPER'S CUNNING ·

A minor incident: a Norfolk keeper employs a cunning ruse. Again it is Dick Townsend who sent me this wonderful tale:

'One November night in 1951 I was on the lookout when I heard a shot on the boundary of my estate. It was about 1.15am and I had a wood situated close to where I had heard the shot. I made my way there, making sure I would not be seen in the moonlight by keeping close to the edge that led to the wood. Very gently and quietly I went into the wood about ten yards, stood still and listened. I wasn't happy. I had disturbed nothing; it was too quiet and my instincts told me I had been seen. No way was I going to get a poacher to walk on to me if he knew where I was; what I did was something you do not learn on gamekeeping courses!

'I thought, pretend you are on the same game as him, so I picked up a piece of stick and held it as a gun and gently made by way through the wood gazing up at the trees as a poacher would do. I had not gone far when I noticed something looking like two stumps near a bush which I knew should not be there. After getting a little closer and looking up into the trees I could see two men who had squatted down trying to hide and I knew they had seen me first. I would rather there had been only one of them, but in those days I did not really care and now I could get close enough to challenge them.

'To my delight I saw a pheasant sitting in a tree about six or eight yards from where they were. This could not have been better: now was my chance to pretend I was after that bird, keeping my back to them until I was close enough to pounce. This I did and made sure I got the one with the gun. It was such a shock to them that the other ran off.

'After taking the gun from him and unloading it we made our way to the Police house in the village. He naturally would tell me no names but just as we got to the Policeman's house the other poacher rode up on his bicycle and said, "I knew you knew who I was and I thought I might get off lighter if I came clean". I did not know him at all, so this was a bit of luck and I can well remember what he said to the Policeman when he made his statement: "I've been a poacher for 25 years but never been had like that. We both thought he

75

hadn't seen us: how the hell he thought of it – it all seemed so natural." I had to smile, for I had not lost the touch!

'I took no cudgel or weapon with me at night in my younger days, but please don't get the impression I was never scared or was bragging or big-headed. This I can assure you is not so, for I have been terrified many times, especially during the war when I spent five years in the RAF. I certainly would not have had the nerve to do some of the things the other men did and thought nothing of. The fact is that I was just not afraid of approaching anyone else at night.'

· POACHING GROUSE IN SNOW ·

In 1943 'Northerner' writes in The Gamekeeper and Countryside *magazine about a form of poaching not usually considered by the average game preserver, In this episode the keeper seems more upset by the fact that he might be outwitted than by the loss of birds, the number of which, even he admits, is inconsiderable.*

'Grouse are supposed to be less vulnerable to ordinary methods of poaching than any other kind of winged game, and that in a great measure is correct, but it must not be thought that grouse are not poached at all in a sneaking sort of way. Such poaching is always indulged in on the edge of the moor which the keeper in charge finds it very difficult to deal with when his boundary runs for several miles. He is also greatly handicapped by the fact that the moor is so open and his coming may be seen when a long way distant.

'A further handicap is that the poaching to which I am alluding always is taken in hand during snow when the outlook for the poacher is still more open and visibility may extend for miles over the moor. No one, not even the keeper, is enraptured by the prospect of long walks over a moor when snow covers the surface and for that reason the poacher is usually free from interference.

'What the poacher prefers is thoroughly deep snow when all the heather lies below it for then he will uncover a small space and expose the heather if he can. This cleared space is very visible on the white expanse. The grouse are certain to see it and there they are trapped with little trouble.

'Another trick is not to clear away the snow but to stick in it plenty of sprays of the most inviting heather which again are apparent to the grouse. It is a simple matter to set traps among these sprays in the snow, and snares placed flat upon it are very deadly as the birds' feet become entangled in them. Such poaching as this can only result in a few grouse being caught and the loss is not serious, but the keeper detests the idea of being outwitted, so I advise that a watch be kept for this type of poaching. It is far more relevant than may be believed when there are dishonest people conveniently near the edge of a moor. When there are many white hares on a moor the grouse will not be trapped, for the hares are the first to see the food protruding above the snow. When they do see it, every atom will be consumed.'

· THE POACHER'S WIFE ·

As this anonymous story sent to me shows, the services of a Victorian poacher's wife extended to more than looking ornamental and disposing of the bag:

'Although both ourselves and our nets were occasionally captured, the watchers generally found this a difficult matter. In approaching our fishing grounds we did not mind going sinuously and snake-like through the wet meadows, and as I have said, our nets were rarely kept at home. They were secreted in stone heaps and among bushes in close proximity to where we intended to use them. Were they kept at home, the obtaining of a search warrant by the police or local Angling Association would always render their custody a critical business.

'When upon any rare occasion the nets were kept at home, it was only a for a short period and when about to be used. Sometimes, though rarely, the police have discovered them secreted in the chimney, between bed and mattress or, in one case, wound about the portly person of a poacher's wife. As I have already said, the women are not always aiders and abetters, but in the actual poaching sometimes play an important part. They have frequently been taken red-handed by the watchers.'

· A GAMEKEEPER'S WAYS TO · PREVENT POACHING

Writing in The Gamekeeper and Countryside *in July 1943, gamekeeper Arthur Bettinson denies that any self-respecting keeper would knowingly trap a poacher by leaving a dead hare in a snare for him to find and be caught red-handed. This might catch the innocent passer-by rather than the real villain and he dismisses the trick as an 'old poacher's tale' – though we know, from much evidence to the contrary, that this might not always be the case. However, he is not averse to more subtle approaches and deterrents and puts close to the top of his list of troublemakers, those who net the stubbles for partridges.*

'Before attempting to net partridges those intent on it watch the ground for several evenings noting where the covies are and, if possible, where they settle down for the night. When this has been done thoroughly they are half way on the road to success. This scouting business may be utilised to bring about their undoing. One matter to which they pay close attention is the location of the bushes placed about to prevent netting and also the way these are distributed. Everything likely to hinder them is noted.

'My idea for dealing with this problem is as follows, and I have always found it successful. There are always on a shoot places where the covies are more numerous than elsewhere, and often they frequent in numbers the fields where the feeding happens to be good. One of these I leave without a bush upon it as if it had been overlooked or perhaps only a bush here and there, not sufficient to be a real handicap to netting. If this field is adjacent to a road or a footpath from which the netters carry out their inspection of the ground, so much the better as they are then certain to see it. All we then have to do is watch that field which is a more simple matter than to keep an eye in the night on the whole shoot. This cannot be regarded as tempting men to poach, but tempting them to do so where they may be easily dealt with.

'When a snare has been set the keeper often has great trouble in watching it with a view to apprehend the man who set it. If nothing happens to be caught in it, that man may walk by it morning after morning and never touch it. You know him from his action to be the offender but there is no real evidence of this. In such a case it is a great temptation to put a hare or rabbit in the snare, but if this is done an innocent man may see the snare and take it.

'A better plan is to disarrange the snare so that it appears as if something has nearly been caught in it and then, depend upon it, the man responsible for the setting will put it in order again. Then you have at once a good case. The idea which permeates the minds of all keepers is to prevent poaching and not encourage it. The keeper who is active about his duties and always on the alert does much to prevent it, but that cannot be said of the lazy ones. There may be keepers who look upon prosecutions as the Indian warrior does scalps but I have yet to meet one.'

· SANS POUCE: MASTER OF DISGUISE ·

In cunning and technique, the notorious nineteenth-century French poacher Philippe Devaux showed much in common with his British counterparts. Devaux had lost one of his thumbs in an accident and was known thereafter as Sans Pouce, the man without a thumb. He was a master of disguise and would often dress up as a wrinkled old crone gathering firewood, and even beg the passing keeper for a few coins – who would often not only hand over his loose change, but also share his lunch with this poor old soul who, had he but known it, was the very one who was stealing his birds. This extract is from the Fur, Feather and Fin *series, vol 1,* The Pheasant *(Longman, 1895) and was written by the Rev H.A. Macpherson. This fascinating series has been reprinted by the Signet Press on behalf of the Game Conservancy.*

'. . . Sans Pouce used to carry his felonious implements beneath his loose, cotton blouse. They consisted of a small, light fowling piece, a phosphoric tinder box and a lantern. He ranged the forest just as he liked but he preferred to shoot over those parts of it which abutted upon the high roads to Paris. Whenever this fellow noted a roosting pheasant he halted for quarter of an hour to ascertain whether anyone else was in the vicinity. If his fears were allayed, he took a careful aim at his victim. His gun was too lightly charged to be heard at any great distance, but he made a rule of shooting at close quarters; any pheasant that Sans Pouce honoured with his selection was sure to fall.

'It was at once picked up, wrapped in a linen bag and stowed away with the gun at the foot of a tree. Sans Pouce immediately betook himself to the public road, and lighting his lantern, marched along the middle of the road talking aloud to himself as people often do when they are alone and nervous. If a patrol or keeper happened to hear the gun fired and ran to the place, he never guessed that the peasant whom he met coming from the direction of the shot, talking noisily and carrying a lighted lantern, could be the poacher of whom he was in search. He was, therefore, certain to ask Sans Pouce for information.

'Sans Pouce never failed to retort that he had seen the man who fired the shot running away in the opposite direction to that which he was following himself. The keeper at once set off in the wrong direction in search of the imaginary offender. As soon as he saw his enemy out of the way, Sans Pouce used to slip back into the forest, pick up his gun and bird and start in quest for a second quarry. He was not particularly greedy and seldom troubled to kill more than a brace of birds in an evening. It was this moderation, as his biographer naively observes, which rendered it so difficult for the authorities to catch him.

'However, Fortune is notoriously fickle and she did not always smile on Sans Pouce. For example, it happened that on a certain Winter's day the keepers noticed the track of a man's shoes in the half frozen snow of the forest. They followed these imprints until they came to a thick holly tree. Here their keen eyes trained in woodcraft saw that the dead leaves which covered the ground had been moved and heaped together with the view of concealing some object which had been slipped beneath the bush. As soon as they closely scrutinised the pile of leaves, they recognised the butt end of a gun.

'The keepers being anxious to catch the knave to whom the gun belonged, proceeded to hide among the holly bushes which stood around. There they remained immovable for many hours when they sought the assistance of their mates. A watch was subsequently maintained for two whole days. At last, on the third night, Sans Pouce himself arrived upon the scene, intending of course to recover his gun. But hardly had he knelt down to pull the weapon out of the brushwood, when the three keepers threw themselves upon him and he was obliged to surrender.'

· CONCERNING POACHING METHODS ·

'Tower Bird', otherwise known as Tim Sedgewick and editor of the Shooting Times *in the 1950s, is scornful of one of the old poacher's alleged tricks which he believes to be so much Scotch mist; writing in his magazine in 1956 gives us a keeper's view of all poachers.*

'There are many "classic" methods of taking pheasants illegally. One reads about them in books written many years ago and they are even recounted today by some of those who contribute to the sporting press. Many of these methods, however, are smiled upon by the experienced keeper and maybe by the experienced poacher as well! It does not behove me to discuss poaching methods in detail, but to give one example of an old and popular fallacy – that of fish hooks baited with raisins. I do not say that a few pheasants might not

be taken in this detestable manner, but I decided to put the matter to test, without the fish hooks of course.

'The birds will peck at the dried fruit and extract the seeds, going to considerable trouble to do so. Certain other "classic" methods might have held good at one period but not so today when intensive rearing calls for a full and energetic staff of up-to-date keepers.

'The internal (I had nearly written "infernal") combustion engine may have improved the lot of sportsmen generally, but it is too often the indirect means of giving keepers a bad headache. The motor poacher in Scotland does things in a big way, for many deer have been illegally shot from and transported by road. The shoot and run method of poaching whether it concerns deer, game birds or rabbits is a despicable form of thieving which deserves a higher scale of penalties.

'Some fifteen years ago we were doing our round of the traps when we stopped dead in our tracks for below us was an unbelievable sight. Instead of the usually empty road and fields we saw a long line of cars drawn up and "bookies" standing up and shouting the odds. On the Flats two greyhounds were necking it after a hare and other hares disturbed by the shindig were galloping off in all directions.

'Passing the cars as though they were of little interest to us we took their numbers and went to phone the Police. We were gone some time and when we returned the meeting had closed down and the caravan gone. However, the Police stopped four cars in a Thameside village. The occupants of one left the vehicle and jumped on a passing bus but the policeman in pursuit was not to be left behind. He too joined the party and leaped onto the same bus, directing the driver to pull up at the police station.

'Fines in this case were a little stiffer than usual, although not nearly stiff enough.'

· POACHING IN THE WAR YEARS ·

The years of World War II were tempting to those not usually thought of as being born to the poaching game. Shortages of meat and the plenitude of rabbits combined with a lack of keepers and the temporary suspension of much organised shooting made for an easy time. But these extracts from a 1943 issue of The Gamekeeper and Countryside *magazine show that poachers did not have things all their own way.*

'Shot Pheasants from Car.
Seen by a woodman-keeper on the Southwick estate coming from the side of the road carrying a dead pheasant, Stephen F. Hamblen of 69, Leith Avenue, Porchester is alleged to have said, "I am only getting my dinner".

'His dinner cost £10 10s, for at Fareham on Monday he was fined £7 for not complying with conditions of a firearms certificate, £2 for killing game without a licence, £1 for firing a gun on the highway. He was also ordered to pay 10s costs.

'Hamblen admitted the offences and PC Toope said the defendant told him he shot the bird whilst he was sitting in his car.'

In the same issue 'A Keeper' discovers a practical use for the Home Guard and its night patrols, although the Home Guard at Sutton Bridge did not deter Kenzie Thorpe for, if anything, the war intensified his poaching activities. In his village the Home Guard were among the worst poachers of them all, having unlimited access to the woods and fields at night.

'The Situation as Regards Poaching.

The poacher like the poor seems to be always with us, little or much poaching going on, serious or otherwise according to the district and other influences. It is pretty prevalent where I am but I believe it is at present limited to the sneaking variety and confined mainly to rabbits. It is to be feared that many an owner of a small shoot not very well keepered runs the risk of losing his last rabbit, for he himself has already reduced them to a very low level and poachers are clearing them right away. On some shoots they have ceased to take precautions against long netting imagining the rabbits to be too few to be caught in that way to make any return.

'However it is possible they are mistaken in following this line, for a very limited catch gives a paying return while rabbits are fetching the prices they are at present. It is very unsafe and unwise to relax precautions against this form of poaching. A great advantage to the poacher is that he no longer has to seek for purchasers of game, for with the present shortage of food almost anyone is open to buy what he can get and ask no questions.

'From what I can gather there is little night poaching going on for it entails too great a risk. Everywhere the Home Guard is very much alive at night and there are few sections of it which do not include a keeper and he is often in command. Men met at night in a field or on the road have to undergo a searching enquiry as to what they are doing and have to produce their identity card. There is little chance of giving a wrong address and getting away with it. The Home Guard also includes many of poaching inclinations. On the whole, poachers do respect the close season for game but this cannot be advanced to their credit, and their forbearance at that time is solely due to the fact that people will not buy game when it is out of season. I cannot believe that this will be the case now, for obvious reasons.

'That poachers move with the times became apparant to me when a friend told me that a man had offered to procure for him live rabbits for re-stocking and this man had no means of obtaining them, except by poaching. Every man has work now and when he is kept busy during the day his inclination to go anywhere but to bed at night is not very pronounced; that is another reason why night poaching is being reduced.'

86

· FOXES AMONGST SHEEP ·

Poachers were more than a match for simple farm labourers – so many foxes among silly sheep, and in this story told by C. Row in 1907 a gang of rabbit netters get the best of the slower-witted Hodges.

'Several of them had been out one night netting rabbits and had caught about thirty couple but it was not practicable for them to get the rabbits into the city before daylight, their cart having failed them. They decided to hide the rabbits and the nets all together in a partially used straw stack on the field. Not considering it prudent to go themselves later on in the morning for the rabbits and nets, they sent the wife of one of them to see if it was all right at the stack.

'She found all gone. Some labouring men having been working in the same field meantime accidentally had come across the rabbits and the nets and having apportioned the rabbits among themselves, very foolishly placed the whole together again – with the exception of one man's share which he wisely preferred to have in his own possession.

'Upon the wife returning home and informing the poachers that all the rabbits and the nets were missing, the men were in a great state of excitement as it meant considerable expense and labour if the nets were not recovered. A consultation was held as to what should be done and eventually it was decided that they should all go and make enquiries of the labourers, and that if they could get the nets back by fair or foul means, all would be satisfied and they would not trouble about the rabbits.

'On getting to the field they did their best to make friends with the labourers, regaling each with a drink of "something short out of a long bottle" and told them of their loss, that they did not care so much about the rabbits as they could soon get some more but they wanted badly to get their nets back and that possibly the labourers could tell them something which might assist them.

'They soon got on the soft side of the labourers who, delighted with their lucky find, very soon proudly admitted that they had found the rabbits in the stack with the nets and as they did not want the nets which were no use to them, the poachers could have them back provided they themselves retained the rabbits, which was, of course, agreed to.

'All went to where the rabbits and nets were, when the poachers coolly commenced to pick up and walk off with the lot, nets and rabbits, telling the labourers to stand back. The nets and rabbits were theirs and they were going to have them as they had caught the rabbits and, much to the discomfiture of the labourers, walked off with both rabbits and nets.'

· ELEPHANT HUNTERS IN AFRICA ·

To depart briefly from the quiet woodlands, heaths and rivers of Britain, here is a poaching method used since time immemorial in Africa where to obtain meat was a rare event in a society which modern technology had barely touched. Today elephants are poached with machine guns, but when the culture was that of the early Iron Age the natives devised various methods of taking the largest land mammal on earth. Sometimes a running noose attached to a heavy log would be placed over a shallow pitfall on an elephant track. The beast would catch its foot and drag the log which so impeded its progress that the natives could catch up with it and dispatch it with spears, giving the village meat and raw materials for a year.

More ingenious and deadly was the falling spear. For this a number of villages would combine all their precious stocks of iron in a joint project which was by no means certain to succeed. In this account the greatest elephant hunter of them all – save possibly Selous – W.D.M. 'Karamoja' Bell describes the device in his classic book The Wanderings of an Elephant Hunter *published in 1923.*

'Of all the devices for killing elephants known to primitive man this is the most efficient. The head and shank of the spear are made by a native blacksmith and the whole thing probably weighs about 400 pounds and requires eight men to haul it into position.

'To set the trap, a spot is chosen in the forest where an elephant path passes under a suitable tree. A sapling of some twelve feet in length is cut. One end is made to fit tightly into the socket of the spearhead and to the other end is attached a rope. The spear end of the rope is placed over a high bough to one side of the path then across it and made fast to a kind of trigger mechanism. It is placed at such a height from the ground as will allow buffalo and antelope to pass under it but not a full grown elephant. He will have to push it out of his way. This part of the rope is generally made fast to a bush or creeper.

'If all goes well, an elephant comes along the path, catches the creeper on his forehead or chest, pushes it sufficiently to snap it off and then down hurtles the huge spear, descending point first with terrific force on neck, shoulder or ribs. I have seen taken from an old bull's neck a piece of iron three feet long and almost eaten away. The wound had completely healed and it may have been there for years. If, however, the spear strikes the spine, death is instantaneous.'

Approach, and through the unlatticed window peep –
Nay, shrink not back, the inmate is asleep;
Sunk mid yon sordid blankets, til the sun
Stoop the West, the plunderer's toils are done.
Loaded and primed and prompt for desperate hand.
Rifle and fowling piece beside him stand;
While round the hut are in disorder laid
The tools and booty of his lawless trade;
For force or fraud, resistance or escape,
The crow, the saw, the bludgeon and the crape.
His pilfer'd powder in yon nook he hoards,
And the filch'd lead the church's roof affords –
(Hence shall the rector's congregation fret,
That while his sermon's dry, his walls are wet.)
The fish spear barb'd, the sweeping net are there
Doe hides and pheasant plumes and skins of hare,
Cordage for toils, and wiring for the snare.
Bartered for game from chase or warren won,
Yon cask holds moonlight, run when moon was none,
And late-snatched spoils lie stowed in hutch apart
To await the associate higgler's evening cart.

The Hut, Sir Walter Scott

RUM OLD BOYS

· THE HIGHLAND POACHER ·

In his book Wild Sports and Natural History of the Highlands (1893), *Charles St John tells of a Highland poacher who saved a girl from possible attack from his dogs, despite losing a chance at a fine deer and the opportunity to blood his young dog. He was careful to cover his face to hide his identity. The Highland poacher always seems to appear more noble and respectable than his Sassenach counterpart.*

'Ronald, a well known poacher, told me that one day his dogs brought a fine stag to bay in the burn close to the house of the forester on the ground where he was poaching. "The forester luckily was not at hame, sir, but the dogs made an awfu' noise *yowling* at the stag and a bit lassie came out and tried to stone them off the beast.

' "I was feared that they might turn on her, so I just stepped down from where I was looking at them and putting my handkerchief over my face, that the lassie mightn't ken me, took the dogs away, though it was a sair pity as it was a fine beast, and one of the dogs was quite young at the time and it would have been a grand chance for blooding him." '

· DEFENCE OF THE SQUIRE ·

Sam Jenkins in 1867 recollects the respect the squire expected and how he lost out by not obeying the unwritten rules of deference but took due toll later.

'Before the Ground Game Act came in the Squire's tenants were not supposed to take so much as a rabbit. The Squire could be generous but he liked his position to be fully acknowledged. Old Jack and I were coming home in a horse and cart and as we came by the turnpike we saw the Squire and his keeper. They had been shooting rabbits and had got quite a number.

'Jack was ever on the lookout for a free dinner and he suggested we should try and beg a couple of rabbits apiece, but young as I was, I didn't like the idea of soliciting what I was used to poaching.

'Respectfully Jack drew his horse and cart to the side of the road to allow the Squire to pass without having to divert to get past. Choosing the right moment Jack, addressing neither in particular, touched his cap and said, "Give the old man a couple gentlemen, please?" There was a quick exchange of glances between Squire and keeper and it resulted in Jack being passed two rabbits. The mute enquiry of the keeper as to whether he should give me a couple also was not met with approval.

'I had not touched my cap nor pulled to the side of the road nor alighted from the cart and I was conscious of his rebuff. "No doubt he gets his own", said the Squire to the keeper.

'When I told my pals of this incident four of us planned a raid. We did not return empty handed, either.'

THE NOTORIOUS FOX TWINS

At the beginning of the twentieth century the Fox twins from Stevenage way were two of the most notorious poachers in the area, but they held a warm place in the hearts of the locals and were mourned when they died. Being identical was a great help to them in their activities for often they claimed mistaken identity or that they had been picking mushrooms. The Fox twins were mentioned in my Poachers' Tales (David & Charles, 1991), but this fuller version of their lives was researched by Gil Gaylor who also sent me some of his own poaching stories. This is a slightly edited version of his account which appeared in Open Field magazine, in May 1990.

'Two brothers rejoicing in the names Albert Ebeneezer and Ebeneezer Albert were born in Symonds Green, Stevenage, Hertfordshire in 1857. The sons of Charlotte and Henry Fox of Ten Acre farm, the boys owed their Christian names to the Ebeneezer Baptist chapel in Albert Street where Mr Fox was a respected preacher. By the time they were ten, the lads had learned every copse and meadow for miles around their home.

'At the age of eleven their education was deemed complete and they began work as casual farm labourers which gave them an ideal opportunity to take to the poaching life which they began by snaring rabbits. The first arrest came in 1871 when they were caught by a gamekeeper shooting pheasants. Mr Fox hired a solicitor for their defence: he pleaded youthful high spirits and they got off. However, a month later the same keeper caught them again and this time they were fined ten shillings, the first of over two hundred court cases in which they were to appear during the next half century.

'In fact Ebeneezer received eighty-two convictions and Albert a hundred and eighteen, the difference being explained by Albert outliving his brother by twelve years. The usual pattern was a fine or a short term in prison and the confiscation of the guns, nets and snares they had on them when caught. Between them they had confiscated over fifty guns which included flintlocks, percussion guns and breech loaders plus miles of long netting.

'Neither married and they lived together in a shack in the woods which they called Woodbine Cottage but gave their address to the Police as "10, Great Wood." The shack was made of turf and boughs with straw on top. If they were poaching away from home they would sleep rough and sell the game locally early next morning.

'In time they got wise to their unique position and poached singly and when caught each would give the other's name. Many a policeman and keeper in the witness box hesitated under cross examination when pressed as to his certainty that it was Albert and not Ebeneezer he had seen running away in the dark. This ruse often, but not always, worked but it became more difficult to employ when finger printing came in in 1904. The twins made local history by being among the first to be convicted on this evidence.

'Some magistrates were harder on them than others: Mr Francis Radcliffe was one of the kinder ones and never charged them more than two pounds a go. Once Albert asked for time to pay and was out that night at his work in the woods, selling the game next morning and paying the fine with the proceeds an hour later. Once Ebeneezer was caught in Hitch Wood having hidden his gun and bag before capture: the case came to Hitchin Magistrates court as usual. The beak asked him what he was doing in the wood late at night and there were chuckles in court when the prisoner replied, "I was there to meditate upon the Baptist book by the light of the moon", and delving into his capacious pockets he pulled out the sacred volume along with a cloud of pheasant feathers. The magistrate was not convinced and it was two pounds again or a month in default.

'In 1915 Albert notched up his century of convictions for then the twins were at their most active. They were in full-time work carrying hods for the new police courts, helping to build the cells of which they themselves were to be among the first occupants. The newspapers referred to them not as poachers but as "Those genial sporting gentlemen who are familiar figures in the local courts on game law summonses". They were by all accounts charming men and regarded by the locals and even the landowners as errant but beloved sons. One landowner made an agreement with Albert that in return for a pound now and then he would leave his coverts alone. Albert being a God fearing chap honoured the deal, but his brother had made no such arrangement.

'The twins never poached on a Sunday and worked out a rota system so that they worked each estate depending on what they thought it could stand. They poached the land of magistrates in accordance with the weight of fines they imposed, a strict man being more heavily hit than a lenient one. The partnership was dissolved when for some unaccountable reason Ebeneezer lost his temper and struck a keeper with his gun and was sent to gaol for ten years. In prison his health suffered and he went partially deaf. He was released after six years, returned to the chapel from which he had derived his name and tried working at various jobs, but his deafness meant that his poaching days were over.

'He was taken to Hitchin Infirmary at the old Chalkdell workhouse where he never settled. In October 1926 he felt his end was upon him and he set off to walk home to die near his beloved woods and fields but he never made it. Half way back to Symonds Green he crawled under a hedge thicket where three days later he was found dead from exposure and exhaustion. Many old friends and enemies came to his funeral.

'Albert continued poaching until 1937 when he was eighty but he, too, succumbed to

old age and was sent to end his days in the infirmary. His funeral was also well attended with landowners, fellow chapel-goers and even the poulterers with whom he dealt coming to show their last respects. It was said that they were popular because they were always so polite and courteous although poaching was in their blood and could never be eradicated.

'They lie buried in unmarked pauper's graves in St. Nicholas churchyard in Stevenage, down in the soil which had nurtured them and had been their source of support all their lives. When the new town was built at Stevenage a pub was named after them. The Twin Foxes; it is no bad way to gain immortality but I wonder what Mr Fox senior, the Baptist preacher, would have thought about it . . .'

· 'UNLUCKY FOR SOME' ·

Dick Townsend is a retired keeper, now in his seventies, from Norfolk. He saw the hard old times and writes with colour and flair about his experiences as a keeper. One day some enterprising publisher will make his fascinating memoirs available to the wider public they deserve. As one for deterring poachers he was enterprising and bold, and even when a young man, earned a reputation as a terror of those who would enter his coverts at night.

This story, relates an episode which took place in 1910: thanks to the sharp nose of his dog Toby and his own keen eyesight, Dick was able to checkmate the traction engine driver who was after one of his rabbits. He had twelve rabbits when there should have been thirteen so he calls his story 'Unlucky for some':

'It was 2.45 on a November afternoon and I had just finished snaring a field for rabbits when I heard the threshing machine coming along the road. It had come to thresh a wheat stack that stood just inside the field where I had left my bike, so quickly I set my last two snares and moved across to the stack to move my bike out of their way.

'In those pre-war days it was the usual practice for the engine driver to get the elevator, drum and engine all set up ready to start threshing first thing in the morning. This way he could finish the stack by 1.30 and be away to his next stack before dark.

'I knew the engine driver well, and so did most of the keepers on other estates where he did the threshing. He had been caught a couple of times for poaching as his job gave him a golden opportunity. He would always be up and about by 4am to get his engine steamed up by 6.30, so he could never be questioned about what he was doing at those early hours by police or keepers unless he was caught in the act.

'I took my bike but did not go home, but hid up and watched until he was ready to leave, then followed him off the Heydon estate as he had six miles to go home.

'Next morning I was round my snares early and got a good catch from the few I had set. There were twelve rabbits, but there should have been thirteen, for one snare was missing and the tell-tale signs told me that there had been a rabbit in it. I took little notice at first for this often happens, and a stray dog, fox or even a cat can be the cause. I was about to move on when I noticed a fresh track which had been made in the morning dew coming from a pit hole about 40 yards away going straight to the snare and then across to the stack. This made me almost certain where my rabbit and snare had gone.

'As I made my way off the field the driver called to me and said, "You've had a good catch, lad," and I replied, "Yes, but there ought to have been another." "Ah", he said, "I saw that get away when I went to the pit hole to 'post a letter' " [answer a call of Nature]. He was no fool and knew I had seen his track in the dew, so this tale would be his best way out.

'He went on to ask me about the rats in the stack and if anyone was coming to kill them. I told him someone would be back later on. In those days the cornstacks would be full of rats and this was before that law which said you had to have netting so they couldn't escape. It was nothing to kill 200 or more from some of those stacks.

'I went home and returned at 11 o'clock with Toby our rat and rabbiting dog and was speaking to the engine driver who was oiling the pulley wheels on the drum when all of a sudden there was a shout from one of the men on the cornstack. "Billy! Billy! There's a bloody dog running off with your dinner bag." We turned round to see Toby a little way in the field tugging and trying to get something out of the bag.

"The bugger is after my dinner," said Billy; but I replied, "Don't worry, he won't eat it, he'll bring it to me, and I don't think it's your dinner he'll be bringing." A few seconds later away came Toby, wagging his tail, right up to me with a rabbit and the snare still round its neck! I gave Billy a long stare and said. "How strange; that rabbit ran straight into your dinner bag to hide up."

'Billy muttered something uncomplimentary about Toby and went off to attend to his engine. When the stack was finished and I was leaving, I heard one of the men say to him, "What did I tell you Billy? I said you'd be lucky to pull the wool over that young bugger's eyes!" '

· A VERITABLE IRISH YARN ·

This yarn was told me by one Paddy O'Reilly, a tenant farmer in County Antrim, as we sat together by the peat fire at the Pheasant Inn. I am unable to vouch for its veracity.

'Wee Mr Jenkins the clerk was a bigger dunderhead at shooting than he was at anything else – and that's saying a dale. Everything, flesh and fowl he'd shot at some time down to the weathercock on Tammas Dorrian's barn that he took for a woodpigeon and never knowed the differs til he heard the jingle of it on the slates. He was a wee, jittery, nervous man with his hands always ready to shoot a couple of seconds or so before his head was. He was as short-sighted as a ten-day-old pup.

'Wee Jimmy Baine came with the errands and told him that there was a flock of wild geese settled in Miss Darby's bog. "I've never shot a wild goose yet," sez he all fidgetin'. "No", sez I, "and ye never shot a tenant farmer yet but you're going to do it now if ye don't stop footerin' with that gun. For mercy's sake put it on the ditch bank there till I talk to ye. Ye know full well that no shot has been fired on Miss Darby's demesne these twenty years."

'It was the truth entirely, for she was one of thim ladies that would not lay a finger on any livin' thing about the place. The pheasants and partridges were as thick as sparrows but divil a trigger would she let be drawn where she had any say. Every hen and duck in the yard had its name on a wee brass ring round its leg and knowed its name too. The best cook she ever had was given a day's notice for servin' up a pullet called Emily Jane. She buried the bird under a headstone in the garden. But for all this Mr Jenkins was out to shoot a wild goose and a wild goose he would shoot, and all the good I did by talkin' was to make him that nervous of bein' caught that he fetched me over four barbed-wire fences and a marsh drain instead of comin' in be the road like a Christian.

'We had just got into the second meadow when Long John the keeper comes by and we hid below the brambles while he passed close enough to touch us. Mr Jenkins as cross as a bag of weasels snatches his gun by the muzzles from where he had stuck it in the briars and at that, bang goes the right barrel. When the smoke riz I looked round for bits of Mr Jenkins and he was standin' there trimblin' and white as a ghost, and feelin' the tails of his coat that was all chattered with shot. "Did you see that? I ruined me breeches on that infernal wire fence and now there's me coat gone, too." "Never mind the coat," says I, snappin' up the gun. "Long John will have heard that shot and be down after us."

'We ran like redshanks until we were safe in the middle of the marsh. "This is all Brown the gunsmith's fault," sez Mr Jenkins getting more savage as he found his breath. "The clumsy, brainless auld fool. First he has the gun pullin' off so stiff that I shot me own ferret, an' me aimin' at a rabbit ten yards to the left of it, and now he has her so light that she goes off if you just blow your breath on her." "Now," he says, determined like, "you can please yourself, but out of this marsh I don't go till I get a shot at them wild geese." "Ye'll be here, then, till the last trumpet frightens them away," sez I, "for the state of nerves you are in you wouldn't hit a goose till the Day of Judgement."

'But as luck would have it, at that very moment half-a-dozen geese rushed out of the reeds. Bang, goes Mr Jenkins and there was a terrible footerin' in the water and when the smoke clears there was a goose scutterin' here and there with a broken wing. You should ha' seen the spangs of him rushing round that bog hole trippin' over rushes and fallin' in holes. He clean forgot his second barrel and had the gun by the muzzles trying to club the bird. In the end he aimed a lamentable blow at it and more by luck than good guidin' put it out of its pain with a dunt on the head which would have felled an ox. The next minit he was dancin' on the edge like a madman shoutin' and wavin' it round his head. "Did you ever see a fatter bird in your life?" he sez.

"'It looks very big for a wild goose," sez I. "Look, there's somethin' on its leg." Round the leg of the goose was a wee brass ring wi' writin' on it which said "Algernon Charles". "Oh, Mr Jenkins, dear," sez I, "Ye've shot Miss Darby's prize gander she named after her uncle, the old colonel." He took a hard look, his jaw fell and I could see the red risin' in his face. "Curse the bird," sez he, lookin' at it. "But, sure enough, it flew: what the divil made a tame gander fly? Anyway, I killed it so I'll eat it, if only for spite."

' "Tie the legs round me neck," sez he, "and let it hang down under me coat. Nobody will notice from a distance." We were well down the back road when round the corner comes Ruddell the huntsman with a pack of staghounds. "He'll see the feet of the gander under your chin," sez I. "It makes no odds," sez Mr Jenkins, "He'll think it's a breastpin. I near blew the intestines out of meself for a gamekeeper the day already and I'll not risk my life for a huntsman!"

' "A fine day, huntsman!" he shouts, as the pack went past. The huntsman touched his hat, never noticin' anything. "That's an alibi established," sez Mr Jenkins: "The huntsman saw me at four a' clock with no goose in my possession." "What's that behind," he sez suddenly. "Oh, it's a straggling hound – go *home*, ye brute!" But the dog had no intention of goin' home, for of a sudden the hound bones the bird by the neck. Mr Jenkins lashes at him wi' the gun. "Let go this minit," he shouts.

' "Easy wi' the gun Mr Jenkins!" sez I, but it was too late. There was a flash and a bang and the next minit the dog was kicking his death thraw in the middle of the road. For a minit or two the two of us stood looking at him, dumb-foundhered. "We have to hide the dog, Mr Jenkins," sez I at last. "Sure the huntsman saw ye with the gun and he'll put two and two together. Wait and I'll hide him in those sally bushes and we'll go to my house and get a spade and bury him. Will ye bring the gander?" "No," sez Mr Jenkins after a long silence. "Bury it!" he says, savage-like, "and bury the gun, and bury me, too, if ye like, for there's neither luck nor grace about me. I'm away for the spade; there's no time to be lost."

'It was wearin' on dusk when we got back. "Gimme the spade," sez he, "and you keep watch; I can handle a spade as well as a gun," sez he, lookin' at me hard. After a bit I slipped along by the sallies to see how he was gettin' on. I could hear the spade goin' as though there was half-a-dozen men diggin' and suddenly – was I bewitched? There was another spade goin' on the far side of the sallies from Mr Jenkins. I keeked through the rushes, and who was it diggin' away for dear life, but Ruddell the huntsman himself!

'The huntsman suddenly heard something and quit diggin'; he looked round him and slipped quietly over to the bushes, spade in hand, and at the same minit I hear Mr Jenkins stop dead. Ye never saw two men so much taken aback in all your life. They just stood there with their mouths openin' and closin' like goldfish in a bowl. Mr Jenkins was the worst struck of the two, for the spade fell from his hand, an' it was the huntsman who spoke first.

'"Mr Jenkins, sir," he sez touchin' his hat; "Ye'll not say anything." Mr Jenkins had not served twenty years in the courts for nothing. "Certainly not, huntsman; I'll not breathe a word of it." All the time his knees was knocking together. "The fact is," sez the huntsman, "that one of my hounds strayed and I think he has been hunting Miss Darby's game and one of the keepers had put a charge until him. I'm goin' to bury him quietly and say nothin' about it." As he spoke he leaned across the bushes and his eye fell first on the grave and then on the spade at Mr Jenkins' feet. The whole thing flashed on him in a twinklin', and him a man of quick temper who had had his troubles before wi' Mr Jenkins.

' "This is too much! To go and shoot my best hound and bury him and niver say you did it is more than a man can thole!" And off he raged like a mill race, while Mr Jenkins jist stood there; but then when the huntsman stopped to draw breath he calls me, and over I come wi' the gander in my hand. "This is one of Miss Darby's prize geese and, Pat, did we or did we not see it in this hound's mouth?" "It's the gospel truth, huntsman," sez I.

Ye could see the huntsman's jaw drop. "Your huntin' in this parish would be done for good if Miss Darby found your hound had killed her prize bird, so I shot the baste and was goin' to bury him here and say nothing' about it."

' "Mr Jenkins, sir", sez the huntsman all crestfallen, "I haven't a word to say: will ye overlook what I said? Ye've saved the credit of me, and the pack too, and I'll not forget it ye. Will ye let bygones be bygones?" Mr Jenkins gripped his hand. "Goodbye," sez the huntsman, "Ye're a gentleman every inch of ye. I'll bury the dog and the goose and be away home."

'We were back in the village before Mr Jenkins spoke again. "We bamboozled him right enough," he chuckles; "I'll get auld Brown to fix the lock and we'll be back after thim geese the first clear night. Nobody would see us." "There'll be nobody see *me*," sez I, "for I won't be there." "Now ye'll come wi me," sez Mr Jenkins, pleadin' like, stoppin' at the foot of the loanin'; "We can't get in a worse hole than we were today, and ye saw the way I got us out of it. There's a full moon in a week or so: I'll go up to Brown in the mornin'. The full moon, then; it's a bargain." An' away he goes hot foot as if he thought the moon might come onto the full before he got home.

' "Don't forget, the full moon," he calls as he goes round the corner. "All right, Mr Jenkins," I shouted back, "The full moon!"

'But the next time Mr Jenkins an' me goes shootin' wild geese together there'll be two moons in the sky – an' another one in the garden.'

· RABBIT CATCHING IN THE ·
TURNPIKE DRAINS

Thomas Todd of Middleton in Teesdale recollects his childhood in the hard times before the Great War when the seeds of a poaching life were sown:

'Our settings off to Woodlands for coals were thrills which were the joy of life to us lads. Sometimes we set off early in the morning, at other times we went at midnight. Boys rarely had money in those days, but if we could raise three pence we called at The Black Horse and had a pint of ale. If a penny was the sum total of all we could raise it was expended on a bottle of nettle beer at Egglestone Toll Bar. Such thirst quenchers were greatly appreciated as the hot roads were inches thick in limestone dust.

'We were always equipped with snares and traps on those journeys. Numerous drains ran under the turnpikes and they were the abodes of rabbits; when we saw them scamper into such places at our approach, it was a simple matter to place traps at each end. It then only remained for us to collect our spoil on our return.

'Often we were pulled up by the police and keepers who were suspicious; but generally we contrived to evade detection by assuming an air of injured innocence. The game we had taken might have been found under the coals.

'It has always been a complaint of mine that police who are paid out of county rates should concern themselves so diligently with preserving landowners' game. Our view was that the rabbits and birds of the air were for those who could secure them.'

· EXCITING ENCOUNTER FOR A ·
YOUNG KEEPER

Dick Townsend describes what he recalls as his most satisfactory encounter with poachers, an episode which occurred when he was the tender age of seventeen, just after the outbreak of the last war. Far from trying to deter them, the youngster was positively wishing them to give him some action!

'Of all the poachers I've caught in my lifetime, no encounter gave me more excitement and thrill than the one I'm about to tell. I was only seventeen years old and raring to go, for so many times I had been out all night with the other keepers just praying to hear a shot pretty near to liven things up, but there had been no luck.

'Well, it was just after the war started in December 1939 and there had been reports of poaching on the estates either side of us, so the head keeper decided to get in touch with the policeman and arrange for him to come out on watch with us five keepers on our estate. This was often done in my younger days, for the village policeman would spend a lot of time with us and be a great help to the keepers; he had far fewer other crimes to deal with than the policeman today.

'We all arranged to meet at his bungalow at 9pm to sort out where we would go and what we would do. This done, Clark the head keeper gave us all a few stiff drinks to help keep out the cold and at 9.45 we set off, ready for anything. We had decided to split up into three pairs, each pair taking their cycles in case they needed to get a message to each other quickly. We paired off so that the policeman and the second keeper in charge were together, then the other two keepers, and I went with the head keeper.

'Off we went to our selected spots waiting and listening, hoping that any minute we would be lucky enough to hear a shot in one of our woods. We had arranged that if any of us heard a shot he would let the others know which wood it came from so we could quickly plan how to deal with it. While we were waiting Clark was telling me what to do and what not to do from his past experiences, if we were lucky enough to have a poacher walk into us.

'We had been there a couple of hours, but not a sound. I was getting a bit depressed for it was quite a good night for poaching, not too bright with a good bit of cloud and a nice wind. I thought, surely this can't be another unlucky night, when all of a sudden there was a 4.10 shot which came from a nearby wood called the Long Belt.

'Clark said to me, "Now Dick; I'm sure George and the policeman will have heard that shot as the wind is right for them and they are nearly as close to the Belt as we are, but the wind will be wrong for the other two, so get on your bike and bring them back to the meeting place."

'I had only got half way when I met them coming along the road and they told me they had heard the shot but it was very faint and they were not sure which wood it was in, but they knew it was our way. I told them it was in the Belt, and just at that moment there was another shot. "Hell!" Harold said: "We'd better get a move on." When we got back, the policeman and George were with Clark and I had only been gone six minutes, so there wasn't much time wasted.

'During that time Clark had planned out where each paid should go and hide, hoping the poacher would come close enough to be challenged. Our orders were that on no account was he to be frightened off and not caught: he had to fall into the trap for it was useless chasing a poacher at night – you are lucky to catch one in twenty that way.

'The plan was for the policeman and George to go to the top end of the Belt where it joined the main road, and find a suitable place to hide and keep watch as the Belt was only 40 yards wide at the top. At the bottom it was 200 yards wide with two rides that led into a main ride which went right through the top. Clark decided he would take the left-hand ride and the other two keepers were to watch the other. We were to blow three sharp blasts on our whistles if help was needed.

'As we were about to go there was another shot but it sounded like an air-gun, not loud enough for a .22 and definitely not a 4.10 so we knew there were two guns. I well remember Clark saying "Now get going: good luck, and don't take any chances." Clark and I got to our place and there was another 4.10 shot about half way up the Belt so they were obviously working their way down. I turned round and whispered, "What about that for a place to hide?" I had seen a hen bird roosting in a larch with the background very dark, caused by a Scotch fir. There was only one place you could stand to get in line with the moon so it looked as clear as day, and that was if you backed up against a big rhododendron bush, which was at an ideal distance for a 4.10 but even more so to grab a poacher if he came to shoot it. Clark said, "My God, Dick boy; it didn't take you long to sus that out!"

'We got into the rhododendron very quietly, making sure not to disturb the bird, and after waiting, listening and straining our eyes for any movement, a pigeon flew over us; it had been disturbed, and a little later we heard a quiet whistle followed by another from a slightly different direction. "They're getting close," whispered Clark, "and it sounds as though there is one each side of the ride, the one on our side fairly well ahead."

'No sooner had he said this than a form appeared on the ride no more than thirty yards from us. He stood still for a fews seconds gazing round, up at the trees, then started to move towards us very slowly, still looking up at the twigs. We knew he would not see the bird very well until he was level with us and then, hopefully, come round to the front of the bush to get a clear shot when it would be a simple matter to put an arm on him.

'Well, he did exactly that, and after he had shot the bird and we knew the gun was empty, as quick as lightning Clark poked his stick into his back and said, "Throw down your gun and you will come to no harm; if not, there's no telling what will happen." He told me to pick up his gun and get back into the bush. This was all done very quickly and quietly.

'Clark told the poacher to whistle his mate to come to him and tell him he had hurt his ankle. The poacher tried to whistle but he could not, he was so shocked. Clark gave him a little dig in the back with his stick which he was still holding there and said, "Have another try". Eventually he gave a whistle and immediately got a reply so Clark said, "Give another, and keep it going until he comes to you". In the meantime we made him sit down on the edge of the bush; he obviously still thought it was a gun in his back while we were just inside, well hidden.

'Not long after he started the continuous whistling we saw the other poacher coming towards us with his gun and a bag on his back. Just before he got to the bush he could see his mate sitting there holding his ankle: "What the hell is it, Boy?" was his remark. "I've hurt my ankle; lay down your gun and have a look. Please, Bob: do as I say, for you're covered and I've got a gun in my back. Please don't run; we're copped, fair and square."

'Harold and his mate were soon with us: "Blast, they've got them both," said the other keeper. "How did you manage that? We were watching one of them about forty yards from us only two or three minutes ago, but he whistled and moved off." We were just about to tell him what had happened when George and the policeman turned up so we were able to tell them all what had happened.

'The policeman said to Clark, "You've done really well," but Clark replied, "A lot of the credit must go to Dick for picking out where to hide." Naturally I felt very pleased at this remark, as he need not have mentioned it. The policeman told us he knew the two men well; they lived only a few miles from his home. He said. "It's a good job you didn't try running after them, for they are 'the running brothers', one a long-distance man the other from 200 yards to two miles, so the chances of you catching them would be like finding a snowball in Hell!"

'They had actually got seven pheasants between them and a skeleton 4.10 plus a BSA .22 rifle which the policeman took charge of. After they had retrieved their hidden cycles he escorted them back to his house to take their statements. The time was then 2.45am and we all made our different ways home feeling very pleased with our night's work.

'As I have said, I was seventeen years old and I am now seventy-one. If I received a fiver for every time during the last fifty-four years that the memory of that night has come into my mind, I wouldn't have to worry about my pension not lasting the week!'

· ELIJAH, MASTER POACHER IN NORFOLK ·

Mark Lorne of Bunwell in Norfolk has a fund of stories about his great-grandfather's brother Elijah, a name which friends and foes alike shortened to 'Lijah. He died when Mark was a child, but Mark swears to me that the stories are true and may be verified by his ancient relatives. The notorious gun "Long Tom" is, he tells me, still working well and taking a toll (see p119). 'Lijah's son Owen is still alive and has inherited the old man's talent as 'an annoyingly good shot'.

''Lijah was a well known character in South Norfolk. His whole family were eminent citizens in his village, including his brother George who ran the village pub amongst other entrepreneurial activities. 'Lijah's claim to fame was that of a master poacher, a fact he had never denied although the local keepers found it hard to establish his guilt. There were times, however, when he was lucky to avoid capture.

'One such escapade happened when he was out in the moonlight after hares. He had been making steady inroads into the hare population in some fields about six miles from his home, despite a heavy fall of snow. It snowed again while he was at his work but the old man carried on regardless.

'It was Sod's Law that on such a night the keepers should be out – they were attracted by regular shots from his gun and made an approach. Keeping a cool head and using the fieldcraft by which he had learned to stay alive on the battlefields of Flanders, 'Lijah was able to find his hidden bicycle and, despite his heavy load of gun and hares, set off apace, intent on disappearing in the snow.

'Some way behind the keepers had found his tracks on the lane. They sent for a pony and trap and some time later they set off, following the marks of the wheels which anyone could see plain enough. 'Lijah pushed on and as dawn was breaking he cycled round the back of The Queen's Head where he hammered away until his brother George appeared. After explaining his problem and that keepers were hot on his heels, it was George who struck on the plan to save him from disgrace.

'The keepers must have been confident of catching their man as dawn was breaking and the tracks were still clear: they pressed on a little quicker in the better light. Then the keeper driving the trap rounded a bend at a trot and was forced suddenly to pull back on the reins.

'Approaching him was a flock of turkeys, filling up the entire roadway as they were driven to market. The keepers sat patiently until the drovers had passed and it wasn't until these had gone that they realised that the trail they had been following so diligently had been completely obliterated. Now it was impossible for them to continue their pursuit, so they gave it up as a bad job and went home in a black frame of mind. Meanwhile George and 'Lijah were driving the turkeys back round the long way to the rear door of The Queen's Head!

'Another time when 'Lijah was being chased he had been unable to put a safe distance between himself and his pursuers. He hid his gun and pheasants in a ditch and cycled back towards the approaching keepers who questioned him closely. 'Lijah informed them that he had passed a heavily loaded man back up the road going *that* way. Thanking him they set off on the false trail, leaving 'Lijah safe to retrieve his gun and bag at leisure.'

· DONALD THE POACHER STANDS · THE SHOT

The Duke of Atholl catches Donald the Highland deer poacher and blacksmith red-handed and teaches him a lesson; but he is impressed nevertheless with his courage under pressure: the matter ends without bloodshed therefore, and with mutual respect. Charles St John recounts this story in Wild Sports and Natural History of the Highlands *of 1893.*

'The day being now broken they had a beautiful race over the moor; but the light-limbed foresters gained ground, the fugitive's pace became worse and worse, he laboured and floundered and was at length seized, all breathless and exhausted.

' "Why, how dare the like of ye come intill his Grace's forest and steal his deer? Ye shall pay the lawin' mon." "Hoot Toot! I'm na thief ava; it's joost for my ain diversion, but ye ha been ower muckle with the Southrons and the likes o' thae chiels aye ca' liftin' stealing."

'The notorious blacksmith was soon taken down to Glen Tilt and brought in the presence of the Duke of Atholl; after a sharp remonstrance, His Grace asked whether he would go to Perth gaol for three months or stand a shot from his rifle at a hundred paces.

'The man said he would stand the shot. "Very well; John Crear, step out a hundred yards." The ground was measured. "Now post the man with his front towards me and give me my best rifle, John."

"The gun was given and raised slowly, whilst the hillmen stood by in a group in breathless suspense, the direction of their eyes changing alternately from His Grace to the man. A long and steady aim was taken; it was an awful moment, but the blacksmith neither flinched nor stirred. At length the cap of the rifle only exploded.

' "Pshaw! Give me another rifle, John and take care that it be better loaded." The second rifle missed fire also, as well it might, it having been arranged, of course, that there should be no charge in it.

' "Well, you are a lucky fellow, for I see your time is not yet come. Give the man his fill of whisky, John; he does not lack courage but mark me, Master Gow-crom, if ever you come after my deer again, my rifle will not miss fire and if it does, the gaol in Perth is large enough to hold you and all the poachers in Badenoch, though ye are a numerous progeny."

' "I wunna say that I will gang entirely wi'out my sport, for I canna aye be wanting venison, but yer Grace shall never find me in yer forest again. There's mony a stoot hart in Glenfiddick and mony a yell hind in the pinewoods of Braemar, let alone Gaick and Glen Fashie and I will leave the braes of Atholl for yer Grace to tak yer pleasure in and never fash them more since ye request the favour." '

· A KEEPER'S CHEQUERED PAST ·

Dick Townsend was not born a keeper. Like many before and since he started on the wrong side of the coverts, but it was to prove a good grounding for him when later he became a distinguished and fearless poacher catcher. It is an old saying that poachers make the best gamekeepers, although Dick saw the light at a youthful age.

'Between the ages of twelve and fourteen I did a bit of poaching myself, climbing down the drainpipe when my poor mum and dad thought I was in bed fast aleeep. This is where I had an early start at night life. I could use one of three things to get my prey: the air-gun if I was well out of the way, my catapult at certain places, and my favourite, the bow and arrow which made no sound at all. Many a time I have taken a pheasant less than a hundred yards from the keeper's house and him none the wiser. However, I had to make sure the wind was in the right direction so that his dogs did not get my scent.

'One dark night I had to come home by road. In our village they used to hold whist drives before the war; these would run from 7.30 to 9.30 and then there would be dancing from 10 until 1.30. My mother and father took part in these, my dad "on the door" and

110

my mum helping with refreshments, which meant they were never home before midnight and this gave me a chance to poach without worrying about being missed.

'I left my house at about 8.30 and took the old route through the gardens and over the Park to one of the outlying woods. I noticed it was quite misty as I entered the wood and after being in it for about half an hour and getting four birds, I realised just how thick the fog was coming down.

'I managed to find my way out of the wood fairly easily, as I knew every tree and there was a ride to follow, but when I got to the Park it was a different story. There were no landmarks to help, everything was blank and I could see nothing. I started in the direction I thought was right, but got nowhere: I had completely lost my bearings. A lump came into my throat and I could feel tears coming. I was really scared not knowing what to do and wishing I had stayed at home, when suddenly I heard music. The lump in my throat disappeared and my eyes dried, for now I knew exactly where to go. The main drive to The Grange came out exactly opposite the dance hall which was only a hundred yards from my house.

'As soon as I knew exactly where I was I hid my birds and came home by road. I dared not risk getting lost again so I picked up the birds the following morning. I have often wondered how long it would have taken me to get home had there been no dance on that night; it was one of the thickest fogs I have ever known.

'Apart from poaching I made quite a bit of money by catching certain wild birds alive. It all depended on the species as to what price you were paid. There were very few birds which came to our Norfolk woods and streams in those days that I could not catch.

'I caught them in various nets and traps and a decoy bird would be used sometimes. My two favourites were the ride net which you would hang across a ride in a wood, and the other, the best of all, was a bridge net. On the estate there were quite a few bridges over various streams which were fairly high and you would get all sorts of birds and wildfowl flying underneath. The net I used was made like a funnel; I made it myself. I would set it over one end of the bridge and then go back to the other side for some distance, making sure to keep well away from the stream so nothing was disturbed until I started netting downstream towards the net. I have caught mallard, teal, widgeon, coot, water rail, snipe, the odd woodcock, kingfisher, penny wagtails, moorhens by the score and many other species by this method. I once caught 43 head in one setting, 31 moorhens, 7 mallard, 2 teal, and 2 snipe.

'Another way of earning money was by snaring rats round the farmers' cornstacks. All my gear was home-made and came from my own ideas. I was born with a gift and was never happier than when I had the challenge to catch something. I used to go to Woolworths at Norwich and buy threepenny rolls of wire and in the evenings would make all my rat and mole snares. One thing led to another and the head warrener on the estate contacted my schoolmaster to ask if he would allow me to go with him and the other warreners on their big "roughing-in" day to shoot rabbits, and how delighted I was when he agreed. It was nothing for three or four men to shoot over 250 rabbits on one of those days.

'When I left school I really wanted to be a gamekeeper, but the people on the estate were no fools and knew my reputation. However, I wanted the job so much that I plucked up courage and went to see the head keeper.

'I shall never forget that day as long as I live. His wife came to the door (he was having his dinner), and I heard him shout, "Who is it?" His wife replied, "It's that boy Dick from

the village." Then in a voice loud enough to wake the dead, he shouted, "Not Dick that bloody bird-catcher!" My heart dropped and I nearly ran off, but he came to the door and asked me what the hell I meant, being round there. I explained to him that I wanted to be a gamekeeper, and asked if he would take me on as his "lad". He said, "You really take the biscuit: you've had nearly as many birds off this estate as we have, and now you come for a job!"

'After an interval which seemed like a week he said with a deep sigh, "Well, I'll see if you are a man who can keep a promise. While I am keeper here you will never poach another pheasant off this estate." I promised him I wouldn't, so he told me I could start work Monday at 12s 6d a week, with no time off. No one could have been more satisfied than I was. I did not want any time off, and remember well that in the first three years I had only three days off from work.'

· SOME NORFOLK CHARACTERS ·

Mark Lorne (if you remember, of Bunwell in Norfolk, p107) recalls some of the odd characters who populated South Norfolk before he was born, and adds another tale concerning the formidable 'Lijah:

'There were several pot-hunters in our area, each of varying levels of competence. These included the head of the local Rabbit Catching Society, a truck driver named George. A keen shooting man, George never managed to connect with a moving target in his life, a fact he never troubled to hide in spite of 'Lijah's constant ribbing on the subject. A measure of his sporting prowess was that he would spend hours sitting in a ditch waiting for a rabbit to come and feed on the carrots he had placed a carefully measured 25 yards from his hiding place. 'Lijah reckoned that he preferred sitting there to being at home with his fractious wife!

'Another local with an eye to the game was Billy. Once 'Lijah found Billy in his favourite ambush for rabbits. Billy had been waiting for a close shot for at least an hour, for he had an open-bored and therefore close-ranged gun; a cartridge had to earn its keep in those days. 'Lijah's solution was to "load up a three-inch cartridge into Long Tom and let him have it", never mind it being at least fifty yards off.

'There is an old saying "honour among thieves", but it was not always the case with poachers. Billy found this out the hard way. 'Lijah and Owen were stalking up to a covey of partridges, on their own ground, for once. With the trained eye of a trench war veteran, 'Lijah noticed a small movement in the adjoining hedgerow: it was Billy, who had also been waiting for the partridges to "draw together" as we say round here, for a puntsman's shot.

'When the covey eventually flushed it was not they who were the target of 'Lijah's gun, but Billy himself who found himself ducking beneath a hail of a double barrel of number 6 shot. Although nothing was said about the incident, it is fair to bet that Billy thought very carefully before poaching again in 'Lijah's territory.

'In his later years 'Lijah would often reminisce about his childhood. One of his tales concerned another brother nicknamed 'Snowflake' who was also something of a shooting man. As times then were hard it was not uncommon for a country lad to take the odd blackbird with a catapult or garden gun to supplement the meagre meat rations.

'The clan's mother was pleasantly surprised when Snowflake entered the kitchen carrying an oven-ready carcase which he left on the kitchen table. It was nothing unusual for him to present her with a blackbird which needed no plucking or gutting. That evening 'Lijah was served up with the bird, and in his enthusiasm to eat it did not notice Snowflake's close interest in watching him fork it down. As he finished eating, Snowflake asked,

"Bet yew don't know what you've just ate, bor?"

"Blackbird?" asked 'Lijah, suddenly wary.

"No," said Snowflake, as all the family fell silent, "Fieldfare!"

· THE LAST OF THE HIGHLAND · HILL POACHERS

In his great work Wild Sports and Natural History of the Highlands, *of 1893, Charles St John describes an old Highland poacher of a type even then becoming harder to find. This man was among the last of his kind.*

'There is another class of hill poacher, the old, half worn out Highlander who has lived and shot on the mountains before the times of letting shooting grounds and strict preserving had come in. These old men with their long barrelled, single guns kill many a deer and grouse, though not in a wholesale manner, hunting more often from ancient habit and for their own use than for the market.

'I have met some quaint old fellows of this description who make up by cunning and knowledge of the ground what they lack in strength and activity. I made acquaintance with an old soldier who after some years' service had returned to his native mountains and to his former habits of poaching and wandering about in search of deer. He lived in the midst of plenty of them too, in a lonely and far-off part of Scotland where the keepers of the property seldom came.

'When they did so, I believe they frequently took the old man out with them to assist in killing a stag for their master. At other times he wandered through the mountains with a single-barrelled gun, killing what deer he wanted for his own use but never selling them. I never in my life saw a better shot with ball. I have constantly seen him kill grouse and plovers on the ground.

'His occupation, I fear, is at last gone, owing to changes in the ownership and the letting of shooting, for the last time I heard of him, he was leading an honest life as a cattle keeper.'

· ENTERTAINING HIS LORDSHIP ·

William Scrope in his book Days of Deerstalking (1897) *tells of the noted Sutherland poacher John More who was paid a visit by Lord Reay on whose land John was used to poaching. His lordship wondered if he might convert More from his evil ways, but he was in for a surprise. In his humble bothy John blew his fire until it glowed, placed a napkin on his lordship's knees and from a dark cupboard produced a small salmon which he spitted on the fire, and a portion of deer heart wrapped in a cloth which he proceeded to broil.*

'Lord Reay asked for a knife and some salt but John replied that "teeth and hands were of little use if they could not master dead fish and flesh, and that the deer seasoned their flesh with salt from the hills whilst the herring could not do so in the sea, and that the salmon, like the Durness butter, was better without salt."

'John produced also some smuggled brandy, and pressed his Lordship to eat and drink heartily, making many remarks on the manliness of making a good breakfast. The chief thought this a good opportunity to endeavour to make a proper impression on his lawless host, and after having been handsomely regaled with plunder from his own forest, determined to act with such generosity towards More as would keep him in reasonable bounds in future.

' "I am well pleased, John," said he, "that although you invade the property of others, you do not conceal the truth and that you have freely given me the best entertainment that your depredations on my property have enabled you to bestow. I will, therefore, allow you occasionally to go to Fionaron in search of a deer if you will engage not to interfere with deer or any sort of game in any other part of the forest."

'More could never tolerate any restraint, and his answer was begun almost before Lord Reay had finished his handsome offer.

' "Donald," said he, "you may put Fionaron in your paunch – for wherever the deer are, there will John More be found." '

· A CALCULATED RISK ·

Stories by and about Kenzie Thorpe are legion, and some of them were told in Poachers' Tales. *This extract from Colin Willock's biography* Kenzie the Wild Goose Man *(1962) shows that the great man was not afraid to take what might appear to some to be great risks.*

'I remember walking four or five miles to a certain farm I had my eye on one rough Sunday night, but when I got there they had a party on. Four or five big cars on the drive and the lights on at twelve at night. They was enjoying themselves, and there was me shivering under the trees with the pheasants all above my head waiting to be shot. And I dursent shoot them with this party there because they might see my torch from the house. I stood there for a couple of hours, and then all of a sudden, the door opens and they start coming out. And you can hear them talking to one another:

' "Good night. I'll see you tomorrow."

' "Good night. Don't forget to ring me on the phone."

'A lot of silly women all promising to meet each other in King's Lynn for coffee on Monday, though I can't think what the hell there is left to talk about, and I say to myself, 'I wish to God you'd get out on it and go, and not stand there gabbin'. Go on, get out on it."

'I've watched the party go, and I've seen the farmer and his wife go upstairs and within quarter of an hour the light go out. Half an hour later I've been round the garden taking pheasants off the trees.

'You never quite get used to starting in on a situation like that. Your tummy is full of butterflies and your heart starts thumping – though you soon get acclimatised once you've had a shot or two. You're soon shooting right agin the house – the .22 with short bullets don't make no more than a spit – and you're dropping pheasants on the front lawn and the gravel drive.

'I can remember one place in particular. Horry and I went there one night to do the job at pheasants, a beautiful rough night. The first two trees were nearly on the front lawn of the house. There were two cocks up the first tree. I shot the first cock and got him in the rear, and he flew towards the house and went straight through one of the downstairs windows. I never saw anything like it in my life. Horry said, "Come on, let's get out of here." I said, "Go on, that wasn't the bedroom window. We'll get them other ones."

'And I just cocked up the old gun and got the other one and we took seven more besides. We had a lovely night, but what-ho in the morning when the farmer woke up and found a pheasant in the house, dead, shot with a .22 rifle!" '

· IN DEFENCE OF GYPSIES ·

The general view of gypsy folk as being the bane of the keeper and of the law-abiding citizen alike comes under attack in this account from an anonymous, but for his day enlightened keeper, who masquerades as 'Had Some' in Gamekeeper and Countryside Magazine *in the early 1940s.*

'On one occasion I went late one evening to move on a party who had camped in a situation handy for poaching, and one of the menfolk told me that they were no poachers and he went on to say that he could prove this to me. It appears that when he went for water at a spring in a nearby field he saw a pheasant sitting on her nest; he took me to this nest and he had spoken the truth. Needless to say I did not move these gypsies on.

'Another instance was when I went to move on a gypsy and his wife. He begged me to allow him to stay for urgent reasons but did not mention what those were. So I made him bring his van close to my house where I was able to keep an eye on him. That night a baby was born in that van, and it stayed for a week, my wife acting as nurse. Since that event you must not say a word against gypsies to her.

'It has always been a puzzle to me whereabouts in their van some gyps conceal contraband they have no wish for the police to see or find. I believe that every van has a clever hiding place where treasures are kept. I have known gyps to be in the possession of pheasant eggs but neither I nor the police could find them.

'There are few gyps who do not possess dogs of some kind or another and many of these are undoubtedly trained poachers which will go off alone and often return with a catch. I have seen them do this. On one occasion a dog returned with a leveret when I was on the scene and it received a good beating, not for catching the leveret but for bringing it in when I was there. These dogs at once recognise a police constable and it is a clever keeper who can hide his identity from them.

'When we caught sight of a gyp poaching, the wiser course was to arrest him there and then, for if you let him go, hoping to serve a summons later, he was difficult to find. He was clever at the disappearing trick, for none of his womenfolk could be found in the van. I have known police to search half a county for a particular van without success and it only had one night in which to make a getaway.

'I never knew a gyp to use a gun for poaching, a net or snare being their preference. Gypsies are clever at telling a sorrowful tale, but it is not necessary to believe them, for many of them are wealthy to a degree unimaginable.

'I have no doubt that when this war is over we shall again see gypsies on the road, and some of them will be wearing medals for bravery in battle. If that is really the case we cannot avoid showing them a little more respect. We cannot expect them all at once to resist the temptation of an odd fowl.'

· LAST LAUGH FOR THE POACHERS ·

'Lijah the poacher had quite an armoury of guns. Here he has an adventure with a hare and a practical joke cartridge; and Mark Lorne tells the tale in which 'Lijah and his notorious gun 'Long Tom' (still being used by the way) earn a reputation for feats of miraculous marksmanship and long range shooting.

' 'Lijah had a diverse armoury, as one might expect from a man who lived by shooting. His best gun was a Darlow's of Norwich, a double hammer gun which he had had made new for him. This was backed up by an old 10-bore said to have come from his brother George in payment of a debt, and 'Long Tom', a 36-inch barrelled 3in magnum of English make. This fully choked monster was famous for its tight shot pattern which, when allied to 'Lijah's marksmanship and an ounce and half of shot, was capable of some amazing kills.

'On one occasion 'Lijah was out threshing for a friend, a local contractor. Threshing held two attractions, one being that threshing men earned more money per day than

ordinary farm labourers due to the seasonal and hard nature of the work; and secondly, that it gave the opportunity to spy out the stocks of game over a great many farms. As usual, 'Lijah had 'Long Tom' with him for he usually arrived early for work to allow himself more time to bag any game which was about.

'During the day Fred, himself a good shot, surprised everyone by offering 'Lijah the chance of a shot at a hare. Fred gave close instructions on where "Sally" was lying in its form, and even slipped him a cartridge for the shot. 'Lijah walked onto the hare and kicked it up. He mounted the long barrel and squeezed the trigger and there was a huge bang and a belch of smoke shot from the muzzle. Once the smoke had cleared and he had steadied himself after the mighty kick of the gun, he was surprised to see the hare running off unscathed.

'Fred stood roaring with laughter behind him and it was not until 'Lijah had inspected the spent case that he realised Fred had supplied him with a starter cartridge for a Field Marshall tractor which they had crammed into a 12-bore case at the farm workshop.

'Although 'Lijah had permission to walk over several small holdings in the area, the urge to stray beyond his boundaries was uncontrollable. It was on such a day that 'Lijah and his son Owen had spotted a cock pheasant in the meadow of a neighbouring farmer. Between them they hatched a plan to bag the bird . . . 'Lijah would stay on the legitimate side of the ground whilst Owen would crawl up the ditch and drive the bird back over him for the shot.

'Some minutes later as Owen completed his crawl, he noticed that the bird had taken flight and was flying back towards him instead of the other way. Unbeknown to him a farm labourer riding past on one of the farm's heavy horses had startled it. Owen, being a star pupil of his father, raised his gun and knocked back the cock's head with a single shot.

'Owen had a good look round before rushing out to gather the pheasant, and it was lucky he did, for by this time the farm labourer had ridden up to investigate the shot. He had seen the pheasant fall dead, and not realising that Owen was concealed in the ditch, had assumed that it was 'Lijah, standing in the open about 90 yards off across the boundary, who had made the longest shot in the history of shooting with the famous 'Long Tom'.

'The story was quickly spread around the local ale houses by the labourer and neither Owen nor 'Lijah would let out the truth. Of such stories are legends made.'

Donald Caird can wire a maukin.
Kens the wiles o' dun deer stalken
Leisters kippers, maks a shift
To shoot the muir fowl in a drift;
Water bailiffs, watchers, keepers.
He can wake while ye are sleepers;
Not for bounty or reward
Dare ye mell wi' Donald Caird.

Anon

HARD
CASES

· DIATRIBE AGAINST THE POACHER ·

In The Keepers Book, one of the Lonsdale Library series, Sir Peter Jeffrey Mackie has little good to say about the poacher. Such a clear-cut approach in a book devoted entirely to gamekeeping is to be expected, but the author did not recognise a shred of merit in even the gentler depredations of Richard Jefferies, moucher who took little but loved the countryside and the birds and beasts that lived there.

'The twentieth-century poacher, taking him by and large, is an ill-conditioned, lazy, drunken and slinking scoundrel, an enemy of law and order without a particle of true sportsmanlike feeling in his veins. As a class, poachers are a set of hardened criminals, careless of everything but their own besotted lives.

'The occasional poacher is a much rarer bird and is the uncurbed expression of the natural poaching tendency which exists in human nature. He may be a farmhand, a village loon or even a medical student home for the vacation. But whatever he may be he is, in the majority of cases, an amateur and not so dangerous as his professional brother who is cast off from honest trades – a grain of the lower sediment of society. He is friend of no man and an enemy to most, and in the majority of cases will be found an errant coward. Remarkably ignorant on most questions, he is terribly acute on all matters affecting the poaching of game, and coward though he be, may be ready at a pinch to get rid of another life rather than risk his own.'

· THE POT HUNTER VERSUS · THE SPORTSMAN

A nineteenth-century pamphleteer who aligns himself with the gentry in such matters, here rails against the practice of pot hunting. The pot hunter is evil, will come to a bad end, certainly beats his wife and is oblivious to the delights of nature around him.

Quite the opposite is the genuine sportsman who chooses to stroll about with his gun in identical but legal manner, leaves beaming wife and daughter, appreciates his surroundings, is smiled upon by nature as he passes and is, in short, in a completely different mould from the vile, evil, degenerate, lying, greedy, rapacious and altogether loathsome pot hunter. The true sporting man has beautiful children, is a better shot, he is conservation-minded, is only out for the exercise and is a saint compared with the pot hunter, whom today we might call a rough shooter, who is engaged on exactly the same pastime.

We are tempted to wonder whether the writer was angling for a shooting invitation from the local landowner!

'Amongst all shooters the most despicable fellow that carries a gun is the pot hunter. Whenever he leaves home in the morning – not for the purpose of recreation or exercise, but of destruction and greediness – his bosom is filled with feelings more base and selfish than even those of night poacher or smuggler. In estimating his character he will be found to be beneath both. The former has to labour hard at an unseasonal hour and has to encounter innumerable difficulties. He is at the same time exposed to the danger of detection and greater punishment. The latter braves the fury of the ocean during the prevalence of mighty storms when death rides upon each foaming wave.

'The pot hunter is a braggart and a coward. No matter who suffers, if he can fill his bag and capacious pockets with game by any means however shabby, he chuckles over his success.

'How different are the feelings of the true sportsman. *He* is accompanied by his faithful dog and leaves the bosom of his family when the morning "opes her golden gates". The blessings of his own offspring go with him as he bids them farewell: the sprightly, the free, the frank and generous-hearted boy, the timid, the affectionate daughter, the beautiful girl who has more power in the glance of her eye than is possessed in the arm of a giant.

'With all objects that shew themselves he feels a generous sympathy. To him there is always the beauty of the season spread abroad with bountiful hand. The true sportsman goes not out for the destruction of game alone; his purpose is chiefly that of exercise and health, the greatest of all earthly blessings. He kills with unerring shot what he conceives to be needful and no more and contemplating the preservation of broods for another season, he returns homewards, delighted with his efforts and his exercise.

'The pot hunter sets out in the full belief that all is fish that comes to his net, or rather that all is game that comes to his bag and capacious pocket: he is animated with one idea, to get as much as possible by what means – only get it! He takes every advantage with which he is presented, whether in the cover among the pheasants or the fields among the partridges. Your pot hunter is seldom accompanied by a keeper. He, disinterested soul, generally selects one of his hangers-on of the tap room, the beer shop or the wharf, the danglers at the skirts of the corn market or the tail end of the butcher's shambles, requiting their services with the generous gift of a mauled rabbit.

'The character of this rouster is enhanced if he can use a stick in a dexterous manner for the purpose of knocking game on the head should an opportunity present itself. The pot hunter stealing behind a hedge will fire at the birds on the ground. He will shoot the hare in her form. When the birds rise he fires both barrels right into the covey, wounding far more than he kills. The genuine sportsman on the contrary singles out his birds right and left and avoids wounding the others.

'The pot hunter has not the skill to kill a cock or bring down a snipe. He has no objection to setting a snare in the morning or to take it up after sunset, exclaiming if it had been discovered, "I wonder what rascally poacher has done this!" He will not hesitate to kill the tame ducks that have strayed in search of food down a drain in the neighbourhood of the farm yard.

'Returning home laden with spoil, he calls into exercise his talismanic powers through the medium and instrumentality of the butcher. Thus a pheasant is changed into a fillet, a brace of birds into slices from the buttock, a hare into a leg of mutton, a rabbit into a thick rib or so, anything and all things provided it saves his weekly expenses.

'Such is the pot hunter! Despicable and despised, the inflictor of torture and cowardly and unmerciful withal, he has no music in his soul.'

· MACCURROCHY THE BLACK-HEARTED ·

Surely the most black-hearted villain ever to poach a deer, and who got away with his hideous crimes only because of the awe in which he was held and the wild country in which he lived, was Donald Currochy Mc-Ean-More of Sutherland. William Scrope describes him in his Days of Deer Stalking, written in 1897. Such a blackguard today would be serving many terms of life imprisonment, but well over a century ago he died a free man and even after his death was able to confound at least one of his enemies.

'Donald Currochy Mc-Ean-More who lived latterly at Hope, was a very noted poacher in Sutherland. Numerous anecdotes are told of this man, but they refer to the great enormities he was in the habit of committing rather than to his lighter trespass against the deer. His acts of violence and injustice were so unusual and savage as to render him an object of universal hatred.

'His family name was MacLeod. He deliberately murdered his nephew that he might possess himself of the adjoining lands of Eddrachilles and he afterwards put to death several of his friends whose revenge he anticipated. He was an expert archer, so ruthless a villain and so ready to slay anyone who offended him, and indeed everyone he could attack whether friend or foe, for at that period when the law was quite inoperative in the remote corners of the Highlands he became a terror of the entire country. The greater part of his time was spent in Dirriemore forest where he was very successful with the long bow.

'His nephew when attacked by him took refuge in a straw-covered hut on an inland loch, but MacCurrochy tied burning pitch and tow to the head of an arrow and firing the roof, set the place aflame.

'The young man endeavoured to escape by swimming but an arrow from the ruffian's bow pierced his heart just as he was reaching the shore.

'MacCurrochy's sheiling was without door or window and he entered by a hole in the roof from which he would occasionally take a shot at a passing traveller. It is reported of him that when walking with his son, a mere boy, on the banks of the river Hope they saw a neighbouring priest on the opposite side of the river. Young MacCurrochy exclaimed, "Oh Daddy, give me your bow that I may bring down the priest."

' "He is at too great a distance from you," said the father, "and you would get us into trouble if you attempted to kill him without succeeding."

'The priest, unconscious of his danger, approached nearer the river and seated himself upon an adjoining stone.

' "Now Daddy," said the youngster, "Give me the bow as I am certain of him." But the old man, still doubtful of his son's success and expecting to obtain a nearer aim, refused this second request also.

'When the priest moved off the boy insisted on being permitted to shoot at the stone upon which he had been sitting, and having hit it with an arrow the very first trial, MacCurrochy complained bitterly of his want of judgement in having resisted his son's desire, and damned himself "for vexing the boy's spirit".

'MacCurrochy was master of a gun which, along with his bow, he is said to have thrown into a deep cavity amongst the loose blocks of stone on the side of Craig-na-garbet, which forms a shoulder of Ben Hope. Many attempts have been made by neighbouring inhabitants to discover these relics, but without success.

'This ruthless villain was buried in a hole in the wall of Durness church by his own direction, to baulk the threat of an old woman who told him, as he lay dying, that she would soon have the pleasure of dancing on his grave.'

· 'NEVER JUDGE A BOOK BY ITS COVER' ·

In his fascinating account of a poaching life The Great Game *(Fieldfare Books),
Harold Wyman describes two different sorts of keeper, one whose bark is worse than
his bite and the other, more to be feared, who 'walks softly but carries a big stick'.*

'Some years ago a friend and I visited a couple of estates to check on the recuperation or
otherwise of the rabbit population, having almost decimated them over a large area the
previous season. Moving along a public footpath we encountered a gamekeeper
accompanied by two fierce German shepherd dogs. We were not left long in doubt as to
his temperament, it was like his dogs, very aggressive. "I know what your game is," he
growled, "If I catch you in my coverts you will wish you had never been born." Our
reaction was one of surprise and indignation: of course we did not know what he was
talking about and were only out for a pleasant stroll.

'That keeper was most incompetent in defending his roosts against marauders, for my
partners and I ravaged his territory every Winter without reprisal. My colleague and I
often wondered at the depth of his sleep for we shot in close proximity to his cottage,
sometimes as close as seventy yards. Add to this the fact that often cock pheasant has left
the roost and flown over his cottage sending out its alarm call as it passed over, never once
were we threatened.

'In direct contrast to the one previously mentioned, this keeper, a Shropshire man, met
me coming down a dead-end lane on an estate under his jurisdiction. "Brandy" was my
companion on this occasion. "I am very sorry," he said, "But there is no right of way down
this lane." I tendered my sincere regrets about unwittingly transgressing boundaries under
his supervision. When I explained my intended destination he quite courteously gave me
directions as to the route I should take. Knowing the keeper was well aware of my
intention to do a little coursing, his repeated glances at Brandy spoke volumes, but never
by word or gesture, did his thoughts become manifest. However, when darkness fell, this
quiet, well-mannered gamekeeper was transformed into a poacher's nightmare. Rarely did
I boast a profitable night from ground under his care, despite the fact that on no less than
three occasions I made a determined effort and never shot more than three and a half
brace.

'I must admit that this short, rosy-cheeked gamekeeper was too clever to allow himself
to be hard hit. A number of rabbit poachers using dogs and lamps were apprehended by
him. The moral of my tale is, "Never judge a book by its cover", for appearances were
deceiving. . . . No keeper has ever taken me while poaching long tails, and I poached
them until I was seventy years of age.'

· A POACHER'S TRAGIC END ·

This tale from an anonymous poacher written at the end of the nineteenth century tells of the terrible end of 'the Otter' who was a noted poacher in Suffolk. It reads like a Victorian melodrama, which I suppose it was.

'As I stood waiting, a black lurcher slunk along under the sodden hedge and seeing the trap, immediately stopped and turned in its tracks. Having warned its master, the two reconnoitred and then came on together. "The Otter" (for it was he) bade a gruff "goodnight" to the enshrouded vehicle and passed on into the darkness. He slouched rapidly under the rain and went in the direction of extensive woods and coverts.

'Hundreds of pheasants had taken to the tall trees and from beneath were visible against the sky. Hares abounded on the fallows and rabbits swarmed everywhere. The storm had driven the keepers to their cosy hearths and the prospect was a poacher's paradise. Just what occurred next can only be surmised. Doubtless "the Otter" worked long and earnestly through that terrible night and at dawn staggered from the ground under a heavy load.

'Just at dawn the poacher's wife emerged from a poor cottage at the junction of the roads and, after looking about her as a hunted animal might look, made off quietly over the land. Creeping close to the fences she covered a couple of miles and then entered a disused, barn-like building. Soon she emerged under a heavy load, her basket as usual covered with crisp green cresses.

'As she eyed the game her eyes glistened and now she waited only for *him*. As yet she knew not that he would never come more, that soon she would be a lone and heart-broken creature. For although his life was one long warfare against the Game Laws, he had always been good and kind to her.

'His end had come as it almost inevitably must. The sound of a heavy unknown footfall on his way home had turned him from his path. He had then made his way back to the lime kiln to obtain warmth and dry his sodden clothes. Once on the margin he was soon asleep. The fumes dulled his senses and in his restless sleep he had rolled onto the stones. In the morning the limestone burner coming to work found a handful of pure white ashes. A few articles were scattered about and he guessed the rest.

'And so, "the Otter" went to God . . . The storm cleared and the heavens were calm. In the sky, in the air, in the blades of grass were signs of awakening life. Morning came bright, birds flew hither and thither and the autumn flowers stood out in the sun. All things were glad and free, but one wretched, stricken thing.'

· LOCH POACHING ·

Loch poaching is notoriously difficult, but ingenious hill men would use an otter, a floating board with flies attached, and nets or lines anchored to each bank, coming back later for their catch. In this account, written in a letter to me, a water keeper described two such encounters; in the second one we might reflect that the poacher was very unlucky.

'One of my most satisfactory captures of poachers was made when I was out late at night on a very still night and heard great sounds of splashing on a lonely hill loch. I suspected netting, but coming down found two men working that deadly instrument the otter. They had a very fine catch of large trout, although the "cast" of the otter was of the coarsest unstained gut and the flies large and coarsely made. How often then had those men been doing that with impunity? Probably all their lives, and how many like them are still doing it?

'It is common for working men anglers to go out in the evening and fish all night, and many use legal methods only, but a big basket conceals many things, as every keeper should know, and if he sees a lonely angler prepare for a night's outing, a return is worthwhile. Trout do take by moonlight sometimes, for it was moonlight when I caught those two poachers.

'Line fishing on loch and river is not uncommon and is very deadly. That enormous brown trout known as the salmo-ferox is a bottom feeder, and an ordinary haddock line baited with herring and large earthworms is used successfully on some Highland lochs to this day.

'Watching once from a hill-top I saw a large trout rise to the surface, swing round in a short circle and go down. Five minutes later it was up again to go through the same performance, and I saw it a third time before I began to "smell a rat". I searched the shore for a suspected line but without result, and having a sudden idea, stripped and waded along opposite to where I had seen the trout. I tripped on a line, and lifting it, found it attached to a stone in three feet of water. Pulling on it I found it went right across the loch, so I loosened my end and went round to find the other end attached to a similar stone on the other side.

'The line now came in easily enough, and what a catch of trout! There were thirty-three of the best, the largest which carried the line to the surface being a ferox, weight 7lb. Haddock hooks on black horsehair and huge lobworms had made a clearance of the big ones. I waited all night for the poacher and got him at dawn.

'The worst loch poaching I ever knew of was done by a sheep farmer; he had what is called a 'scringe' net and used it on the lonely lochs by moonlight. The man is probably netting away in security to this day for I only found out he was doing it by chance ...'

· 'BUCK' THE LADY POACHER ·

Lady poachers were nothing new in the hard old days. This formidable woman known as 'Buck' was a match for any man who stalked the coverts at night: her knowledge of rabbits was encyclopaedic and she had 'done time' in prison for poaching offences. However, she emerges as a strong and resolute character who did not waste her ill-gotten profits. The extract which describes her here is taken from George A.B. Dewar's The Faery Year.

'For generations to come the deeds of "Buck", our poacher in petticoats, will be discussed in the group of villages where her grotesque figure was so familiar. Rabbits are great talk for hamlet folk and about this strange woman there was a very romance of rabbits. To many sportsmen one rabbit is very like another. I never stop to criticise a rabbit that I shot, being for one thing unable to judge by finger or eye its merit or demerit for the table. But in thorough rabbit districts the cottager is quite a connoisseur in conies. When a rabbit slightly above the average in size of fitness is shot or snared, it is often remarked on. Village sportsmen can hardly shoot a rabbit without discovering its excellence – "a fine rabbit, too", is the verdict. Others who do not shoot or beat have something to tell each other about the rabbits in a particular field or spinney.

'This interest in rabbits of itself might explain the fame of "Buck"; but besides, hers was a strong, singular personality. She had retired from the business some time before she died about a year ago, but her fame had scarcely lessened in the neighbourhood. Today, when the leaf is off and rabbit shooting in full swing, we naturally talk of her.

'This resolute poacher had been to gaol two or three times for refusing or being unable to pay her fines, but she was no wastrel. She tried to keep the bit she made from poaching but her first husband was thriftless and once, when she was in gaol, he sold and drank away the pigs which she had bought out of her poaching profits. "Buck" was the daughter of a gamekeeper and learned most that she knew of the game and snaring it by going to the woods with her father in girlhood. She was a match for any male poacher in the wiring game, furred and feathered, and worked her ferrets with skill.

'She had a gun and nerve to go into the copse after dark to shoot roosting pheasants. The sound of the pheasant poacher's gun at nightfall used to be heard more often than it is today. The risk was not so great as one might suppose, save where keepers and watchers were numerous. The old muzzle loader was carried in pieces hidden deep in coat pockets and not fitted together until the wood was entered. It did not make much noise for the paocher loaded it very lightly with powder. She was near her game so a full charge was not needful. The result was a kind of muffled report and in the midst of woods I noticed that this sound was hard to locate.

'Charles Waterton, to torment the poachers and to waste their powder, had wooden bird dummies nailed on his trees. I doubt whether a complete poacher like "Buck", nothing if not wood crafty, could be cheated so.'

· A POLICEMAN'S NARROW ESCAPE ·

Noel 'Tim' Sedgewick was a noted editor of The Shooting Times *magazine in the fifties and sixties. In this extract from the magazine in the mid sixties he describes what started as a run-of-the-mill encounter but ended with a narrow squeak for the policeman.*

'On the very last estate in Essex where I helped as a lad to rear a few pheasants, a keeper was killed by a poaching gang.

'Some years later, on this same estate, the owner and myself were walking quietly outside a rhododendron covert one moonlight night when we heard the sound of digging. Gingerly approaching the spot we came to a clearing where a man and two powerful dogs were engaged on a large burrow. As we broke cover one of the dogs sprang at my companion seizing him by the leg. Fortunately he was wearing wellingtons; nevertheless his leg received bad brusing before I could beat off the savage brute.

'The man was identified as having recently been released from a mental institution and because of his behaviour, was eventually sent back there. However, having fetched the local Policeman and given the miscreant in charge and having driven him to the lockup, the three of us returned to the house where our host poured out drinks in the gun room and took from his pocket the revolver he was wont to carry when out after poachers at night.

'How it happened we were never certain, but there came a shattering roar and a bullet passed within an inch of the representative of the Law, embedding itself in a wall behind him. Thus even a man most careful in the handling of lethal weapons can never prove infallibly so!'

· A POLICEMAN AVOIDS TROUBLE ·

This is a tale again from Richard Fawcett's Pennine Poacher *concerning grouse poaching, and a wise policeman who learned just in time that discretion is the better part of valour.*

'On one occasion, about the 7 or 8 August just before the Grouse Shooting Act came in, my pal and I had netted thirteen brace of birds on Raven Hills. As we made our way homeward before day broke we jokingly commented that we had secured a very unlucky number. We were nevertheless well satisfied with our work and had already got a nice stock together to pass into the hands of the game dealer.

'We had just reached the point on the bridge where a deep drop is separated from the roadway by a low stone wall. Where the polis came from is still a mystery, but he loomed in front of us and if he were inclined, it was a catch. There was no chance of hiding from him and as I realised this I was overwhelmed with a loathsome disgust for him whom I then regarded as a paid bully.

'Our pockets were bulging, and we were twice our normal width which was naturally generous at any time. During those few strides which quickly lessened the distance between us, I was seized with the fiendish impulse to clutch him between the buttocks in what was known as the Steadman grip and hurl him over the parapet into the stream below.

'The policeman struck me a sharp blow against my pocket with his stick. With a curse I crouched to grab him, and believe me, that man's fate was sealed even if his weight was sixteen stones. I was too enraged to think of the consequences – my only thought was to smash him. Whether he was seized with panic I never knew, but he stepped quickly backwards and to one side. "Guid neet, Tom," he said and went on.

'If that man sensed what was coming he proved to be a very wise chap indeed, because he saved himself from serious injury and me a term of imprisonment at least. I owe that policeman a debt of gratitude for getting out of my way – quickly.

'I was scared, but it was at myself. It was not very often, happily, that became possessed of the devil.'

· THE POACHING GAMEKEEPER ·

A Victorian moralist warns of the risks of allowing a keeper to carry a gun. In the extract below he tells landowners to be on their guard against a rarely encountered individual (or was he more common than we are led to believe?), the poaching gamekeeper, who finds himself with temptation in his path or seeks to supplement his income by taking advantage of his master's shooting guests. His worry about the poaching keeper amounts almost to a paranoia; one wonders whether he had had a bad experience in this way.

'It is said that there are tricks in every trade and assuredly the keeper and the poacher, in pursuing each his respective calling, are not free from this imputation. There are, no doubt, *many* honest keepers, but it must be apparent that the occupation of a keeper affords him innumerable opportunities for the commissioning of dishonest actions. He has the whole range of the estate, and if he is mercenary and has opened communication with the conveyancers, which he can do with perfect safety, particularly if the spot on which he resides be adjoining a turnpike road, he can carry on a secret trade in game to an almost unlimited extent.

'The practice of allowing a keeper to carry a gun is one of the means by which he can most readily turn things to his own advantage. It has no doubt a very plausible appearance, for are there not vermin on the estate to be destroyed? Must not his master's table be supplied with game? But alas! It too often happens that the gamekeeper's eyes from some cause or other become confused to a degree that he is apt to mistake a hare for a weasel and a pheasant for a hawk. In consequence of the prevalence of this unfortunate failing, many gentlemen will not allow their keepers to carry a gun.

'But still, if they are so disposed, there are a thousand other means at their command for killing an unlimited quantity of game by nets, traps and snares. But it is not only by the unlawful use of his gun that the gamekeeper seeks to augment his income. He has other means at his command which, though not so nefarious from a moral point of view, are no less deserving of notice and reprehension.

'Should, for instance, any gentleman who visits his master for a day's shooting be known by the keeper to be rather chary of cash, he takes him to that part of the estate where there is the least game or if he has particular orders to take him to the best preserves, knowing him to be a dead shot, he contrives to give the dogs of the unsuspicious stranger a good draught or two of buttermilk before starting which has the effect of spoiling their noses and of making them point where there are no birds. This is to the great mortification of the visitor who wonders what can be the reason that his dogs are so much at fault.

'His worthy companion the while declares that they are not worth their keep or that the man who broke them knew nothing of his business. Besides this there are other means to thwart the sport of the stranger by marking wrong or throwing the dogs off the immediate locality of game. Of course the conduct of the keeper is the reverse of this if the gentleman pays well!'

· THE IRON WOLF ·

The mantrap, sometimes known as the iron wolf, has long been outlawed but its very existence indicates the lengths to which keepers and landowners would go to preserve their game. In this story from the 1880s sent to me by a correspondent, a poacher describes a narrow escape and a keeper falling 'into the pit which he had digged', a case of the biter bit.

'I remember a cruel incident from my earliest poaching days which had a very different ending from what its author intended. A young keeper had made a wager that he would effect my capture within a certain number of days and my first intimation of this fact was a sickening sight which I discovered in passing down a woodland glade just about dawn on a bright December morning. I heard a groan and a few yards in front saw a man stretched out on the ride. His clothes were covered with hoar frost, he was drenched in blood and the poor fellow's pale face showed me that of the keeper.

'He was held fast in a mantrap which had terribly lacerated his lower limbs. He was conscious but quite exhausted. Although in great agony he suffered me to carry him to a neighbouring hayrick from whence we removed him to his cottage. He recovered slowly and the mantrap which he had set the night before was, I believe, the last ever used in that district.'

139

· THE GRASS FAMILY: DYNASTY · OF GAMEKEEPERS

The name Grass was one feared, hated and respected in the poaching world. The Grasses were the largest clan of gamekeepers in the history of the profession and they spread about the land to estates great and small, passing on the skills to successive generations. They must have had the blood in them.

Not all of them came directly to gamekeeping, for a number were poachers first; this was a common enough transition, and it was often said that good poachers made better gamekeepers. An early Grass was convicted of rabbit stealing in 1805 and received not only six months in prison but was whipped in the town square. Other Grasses were variously imprisoned and transported. One was an expert at robbing rabbit traps, his trick being to replace the rabbit with a torn off leg to make it appear as if the trap had been raided by a fox or badger.

Even when they turned to keepering, violence was never far away in those wild days. Robert Grass was so badly beaten by poachers that he could not work again, while Jack Grass was tied to a tree by a gang, tortured and threatened with death, to be saved only by the timely arrival of his son with a dog.

Their attitude to small, local poachers was often a lenient one. Such men were a good source of information about more serious raiders, and besides, some estate owners disliked the adverse publicity of court cases brought against tenants who in one case were tried by the keeper, had their gear confiscated and were made to pay £1 for charity.

The Grass family enjoyed between them many generations of successful gamekeeping and before that poaching, and their combined knowledge would undoubtedly amount to a book of many volumes about both subjects. There could have been few things that they had not encountered in a span of years which must have amounted to several hundred.

For example, there was the unusual case of the egg stealers who could be such a pest. Game eggs were always in demand and fetched a few pence from the publican who often acted as 'fence' and passed the eggs on to game rearers. On one occasion a nest of poisoned eggs was left out to kill carrion crows, a trick once commonly used but now strictly outlawed, as is the leaving of any form of poisoned bait.

In those tough old days an egg stealer found the nest and took the eggs, unaware of their deadly contents. Feeling peckish on the way home he sucked one of them, and died from strychnine poisoning. The keeper was charged with manslaughter but freed on a technicality. While poisoned flesh and fowl were specified in the legislation there was no word about eggs so, not for first time, did a Grass find luck on his side.

No poaching book would be complete without a brief reference to such a famous family.

Now was the game destroyed and not a hare
Escaped at least the danger of the snare;
Woods of their feathered beauty were bereft,
The beauteous victims of the silent theft;
The well-known shops received a large supply
That those who could not kill at least might buy.

James was enraged, enraged his lord, and both
Confirmed their threatening with a vengeful oath:
Fresh aid was sought – and nightly on the lands
Walk'd on their watch in strong determined bands:
Pardon was offer'd, and a promised pay
To him who would the desperate gang betray.
Not fail'd the measure – on a certain night
A few were seized – the rest escaped by flight;
Yet they resisted boldly ere they fled,
And blows were dealt around and blood was shed;
Two groaning helpers on the earth were laid,
When more arrived the lawful cause to aid:
The four determined men were seized and bound,
And Robert in this desperate number found:
In prison fettered, he deplored his fate,
And cursed the folly he perceived too late.

The Rev George Crabbe, 1819

GREVIOUS
BODILY
HARM

· THE BORDER BALLADS ·

The Border Ballads tell of the running battles fought between the wild men of lowland Scotland and the equally wild men of northern England. They spent their time raiding each other's cattle, burning crops, sacking castles, pillaging, forming dangerous liaisons with the daughters/sons of the enemy and dashing back and forth in quick strike raids, reiving and 'little local difficulties'. There can be few acres of the Border lands which have not had blood shed upon them.

One of the most famous was the battle of Chevy Chase, in which a raiding party led by the Duke of Northumberland poached a herd of deer in the Cheviots. He did this as much to cock a snook at Douglas who claimed them as his – as much as anyone could be said to own anything in those lawless times. Douglas responded to the insult and came down in force to repel the intruders, and the battle of Otterburn, in which both of them lost their lives, was the result.

This was the poaching affray to end them all, a dispute which leaves nowhere the most bloodthirsty Victorian confrontation in woodlands between keepers and poachers, a tea-party by comparison. Some of the language is archaic, but this is a very old yarn, passed down by poets and singers through the ages and no doubt it has been improved in the telling – what good story has not?

· THE BATTLE OF CHEVY CHASE ·

Anon.

Percy of Northumberland vows to hunt the deer of Cheviot in spite of the threat of the mighty Douglas; on a Monday he sets to work with 1,500 archers hidden by the passes, and sends his beaters though the woods to drive the deer to the waiting bowmen.

Fytte I

I

THE Percy out of Northumberland,
   An avow to God made he
That he would hunt in the mountains
   Of Cheviot within days three,
In the maugre of doughty Douglas,
   And all that e'er with him be.

II

The fattest harts in all Cheviot
   He would kill and carry away. –
'By my faith,' said the doughty Douglas again,
   'I will let that hunting if I may!'

III

Then the Percy out of Banborowe came,
   With him a mighty meinye,
With fifteen hundred archérs bold
   Chosen out of shires three.

IV

This began on a Monday at morn,
   In Cheviot the hills so hye;
The child may rue that is unborn,
   It was the more pitye.

V

The drivers through the woodès went
   [All] for to raise the deer,
Bowmen bicker'd upon the bent
   With their broad arrows clear.

   maugre] despite.   let] hinder.   meinye] company   bicker'd] attacked, skirmished.   bent] rough grass.

144

The greyhounds help to push the beasts forward and the archers shoot well. By midday they have killed a hundred deer and were busy with the gralloch and blowing the 'mort' as was the custom in medieval venery. Percy is disappointed that his enemy has not turned up, but the words are still on his lips when a squire looks up and sees the Douglas approaching with a large, well armed company.

VI

Then the wild thoro' the woodès went
   On every sidè shear;
Grayhounds thoro' the grevès glent
   For to kill their deer.

VII

This began on Cheviot the hills abune
   Early on a Monenday;
By that it drew to the hour of noon
   A hundred fat harts dead there lay.

VIII

They blew a mort upon the bent,
   They 'sembled on sidès shear;
To the quarry then the Percy went
   To the brittling of the deer.

IX

He said, 'It was the Douglas' promise
   This day to meet me here;
But I wist he would fail, verament!'
   – A great oath the Percy sware.

X

At the last a squire of Northumberland
   Lookèd at his hand full nigh;
He was ware o' the doughty Douglas coming,
   With him a great meinye.

XI

Both with speär, bill and brand, –
   'Twas a mighty sight to see;
Hardier men both of heart nor hand
   Were not in Christianè.

  wild] game, deer.   shear] several   grevès]
groves.   glent] glanced, darted.   mort] death of
the deer.   quarry] dead game.   brittling] cutting
up.

Douglas has about 2,000 men who had come along the Tweed to the meeting place. He is well armed, and demands of Percy what right he has to take the deer. Percy gives a defiant answer and points out that not only has he killed the best beasts in the forest but he means to take them home with him. Douglas vows that one of them will die for this.

XII

They were twenty hundred spearmen good,
  Withouten any fail:
They were born along by the water o' Tweed
  I' the boun's o' Teviotdale.

XIII

'Leave off the brittling of deer,' he said;
  'To your bows look ye take good heed,
For sith ye were on your mothers born
  Had ye never so mickle need.'

XIV

The doughty Douglas on a steed
  Rode all his men beforn;
His armour glitter'd as did a gleed,
  Bolder bairn was never born.

XV

'Tell me whose men ye are,' he says,
  'Or whose men that ye be;
Who gave you leave in this Cheviot chase
  In the spite of mine and of me?'

XVI

The first man that him answer made
  It was the good Lord Percye:
'We will not tell thee whose men we are,
  Nor whose men that we be;
But we will hunt here in this chase
  In the spite of thine and of thee.

XVII

'The fattest harts in all Cheviot
  We have kill'd, to carry away.' –
'By my troth,' said the doughty Douglas again,
  'The one of us dies this day.

boun's] boundaries.   gleed] live coal.   bairn] fighting man.

146

The Northumbrians fire a volley of arrows and account for 140 Scots at one discharge. But Douglas was a shrewd tactician and he keeps his head: he divides his force into three and cuts through the English lines. The bowmen have to drop their bows and take to their swords for the close work.

XXIII

That day, that day, that dreadful day! –
  The first fytte here I find:
An you'll hear any more o' the hunting of Cheviot,
  Yet there is more behind.

Fytte II
XXIV

The Englishmen had their bows y-bent,
  Their hearts were good enow;
The first of arrows that they shot off
  Seven score spearmen they slew.

XXV

Yet bides the Earl Douglas upon the bent,
  A captin good enoghe;
And that was seenè verament,
  For he wrought them both woe and wouche.

XXVI

The Douglas parted his host in three,
  Like a chief chieftain of pride;
With surè spears of mighty tree
  They came in on every side;

XXVII

– Throughè our English archery
  Gave many a woond full wide;
Many a doughty they gar'd to dye,
  Which gainèd them no pride.

XXVIII

The Englishmen let their bowès be,
  And pull'd out brands that were bright;
It was a heavy sight to see
  Bright swords on basnets light.

fytte] division of a ballad.   wouche] evil.
tree] timber.   doughty] doughty man.   basnets]
steel caps.

In the melée Douglas and Percy meet and fight until the blood sprays like rain from their helmets. Douglas offers Percy a truce and says he will take him to the Scottish court where he will be nobly treated. Percy refuses as he is not a man for yielding.

XXIX

Thoro' rich mail and manoplie
   Many stern they struck down straight;
Many a freyke that was full free
   There under food did light.

XXX

At last the Douglas and the Percy met,
   Like to captains of might and of main;
They swapt together till they both swat
   With swordès of fine Milan.

XXXI

These worthy freykès for to fight
   Thereto they were full fain,
Till the blood out of their basnets sprent
   As ever did hail or rain.

XXXII

'Yield thee, Percy,' said the Douglas,
   'And i' faith I shall thee bring
Where thou shalt have an Earl's wages
   Of Jamie out Scottish king.

XXXIII

'Thou shaltè have thy ransom free,
   – I hight thee here this thing;
For the manfullest man thou art that e'er
   I conquer'd in field fighting.'

XXXIV

But 'Nay', then said the lord Percye,
   'I told it thee beforn
That I would never yielded be
   To man of a woman born.'

   manoplie] long gauntlet.   stern] stern men, war-
riors.   freyke] bold fellow.   swapt] smote.
swat] sweated.   sprent] spurted.   hight] promise.

*At that moment a chance arrow strikes Douglas and transfixes him: he dies,
urging his men to fight on. Percy is sad that such a noble adversary should
end thus. Sir Hugh Montgomery sees his leader fall and battles through the
press to get at Percy.*

XXXV
With that an arrow came hastily
   Forth of a mighty wane;
And it hath stricken the Earl Douglas
   In at the breastè-bane.

XXXVI
Thoro' liver and lungès both
   The sharp arròw is gone,
That never after in his life-days
   He spake mo words but one:
'Twas, 'Fight ye, my merry men, whiles ye may,
   For my life-days bin gone!'

XXXVII
The Percy leanèd on his brand
   And saw the Douglas dee;
He took the dead man by the hand,
   And said, 'Woe is me for thee!

XXXVIII
'To have sav'd thy life I'd have parted with
   My lands for yearès three,
For a better man of heart nor of hand
   Was not in the north countrye.'

XXXIX
[All this there saw] a Scottish knight,
   Sir Hugh the Montgomerye:
When he saw Douglas to the death was dight,
   Through a hundred archerye
He never stint nor he never blint
   Till he came to the lord Percye.

wane] host, multitude.   dight] done, doomed.
stint] stayed.   blint] stopped.

He strikes at Percy with his spear so savagely that the blade stands out a full yard beyond his body. An English archer sees this and shoots Sir Hugh Montgomery so powerfully that the goose feathers of his arrow are drenched with his heart's blood. The battle has gone on all afternoon and is by no means over.

XL

He set upon the lord Percỳ
   A dint that was full sore;
With a surè spear of a mighty tree
   Thro' the body him he bore,
O' the t'other side that a man might see
   A large cloth-yard and more.

XLI

An archer of Northumberland
   Saw slain was the lord Percye:
He bare a bent bow in his hand,
   Was made of a trusty tree.

XLII

An arrow that was a cloth-yard long
   To the hard steel halèd he,
A dint that was both sad and sair
   He set on Montgomerye.

XLIII

The dint it was both sad and sair
   That he on Montgomerye set;
The swan-feathers that his arrow bare
   With his heart-blood they were wet.

XLIV

There was never a freykè one foot would flee,
   But still in stoure did stand;
Hewing on each other, while they might dree,
   With many a baleful brand.

XLV

This battle began in Cheviot
   An hour before the noon,
And when the even-song bell was rung
   The battle was not half done.

   dint] stroke, lunge.   halèd] pulled.   stoure]
press of battle.   dree] endure.

The battle rages on until the moon rises and the combatants stop through exhaustion. Of the 1,500 English only 73 survive and 55 Scots. There is a list of the noblest of the dead including Witherington who, when both his legs were cut off fought on on his stumps!

XLVI

They took [their stand] on either hand
   By the [lee] light of the moon;
Many had no strength for to stand
   In Cheviot the hills abune.

XLVII

Of fifteen hundred archers of England
   Went away but seventy-and-three;
Of twenty hundred spearmen of Scotland
   But even five-and-fiftỳ.

XLVIII

There was slain with the bold Percye
   Sir John of Agerstoune,
Sir Roger, the hendè Hartley,
   Sir William, the bold Herone.

XLIX

Sir George, the worthy Loumlye,
   A knight of great renown,
Sir Ralph, the richè Rabye,
   With dints were beaten down.

L

For Witherington my heart was woe
   That ever he slain should be:
For when both his legs were hewn in two
   Yet he kneel'd and fought on his knee.

LI

There was slayn with the doughty Douglas
   Sir Hugh the Montgomerye,
Sir Davy Lambwell, that worthy was,
   His sister's son was he.

lee] fair, bright.   hendè] courteous, gentle.

The next day biers are made of birch and hazel and weeping widows come to take away their menfolk. King James of Scotland rails that he has lost the best man in his kingdom. Henry the Fourth while sad at the loss, says he has a hundred other captains as good as Percy.

LII

Sir Charles a Murray in that place,
   That never a foot would flee:
Sir Hew Maxwell, a lord he was,
   With the Douglas did he dee.

LIII

So on the morrow they made them biers
   Of birch and hazel so gray;
Many widows with weeping tears
   Came to fetch their makes away.

LIV

Teviotdale may carp of care,
   Northumberland may make moan,
For two such captains as slain were there
   On the March-parts shall never be none.

LV

Word is come to Edinboro',
   To Jamie the Scottish King,
Earl Douglas, lieutenant of the Marches,
   Lay slain Cheviot within.

LVI

His hands the King did weal and wring,
   Said, 'Alas! and woe is me!
Such another captain Scotland within
   I' faith shall never be!'

LVII

Word is come to lovely London
   To the fourth Harry, our King,
Lord Percy, lieutenant of the Marches,
   Lay slain Cheviot within.

makes] mates.   carp] talk.   weal] clench.

Thus ends the tale of the bloodiest poaching affray in all time and the poet is surprised that the rivers of Cheviot do not to this day run red with blood.

LVIII

'God have mercy on his soul,' said King
Harry,
  'Good Lord, if thy will it be!
I've a hundred captains in England,' he said,
  'As good as ever was he:
But Percy, an I brook my life,
  Thy death well quit shall be.'

LIX

And as our King made his avow
  Like a noble prince of renown,
For Percy he did it well perform
  After, on Homble-down;

LX

Where six-and-thirty Scottish knights
  On a day were beaten down;
Glendale glitter'd on their armour bright
  Over castle, tower and town.

LXI

This was the Hunting of the Cheviot;
  That e'er began this spurn!
Old men, that known the ground well,
  Call it of Otterburn.

LXII

There was never a time on the March-partès
  Since the Douglas and Percy met,
But 'tis marvel an the red blood run not
  As the reane does in the street.

LXIII

Jesu Christ! our balès bete,
  And to the bliss us bring!
This was the Hunting of the Cheviot:
  God send us all good ending!

  brook] retain.   Glendale] one of the six
'wards' of Northumberland. Homildon was
here. spurn] fray (!).   reane] gutter-
   balès] woes.   bete] better, relieve.

· A MORTAL AFFRAY ·

There is no doubt that some fearful confrontations took place in Victorian days when keepers and desperate poachers clashed in the moonlit avenues of the woodlands. This long extract, well worth using in entirety, is taken from a book published in 1866 called Sporting Sketches at Home and Abroad *by the 'Old Bushman', otherwise Horace William Wheelwright. He paints a colourful, contemporary picture of country life in those far-off times and recounts vividly this eye-witness tale of the fierce poachers in his little village and the running battle they had with the keeper Johnson.*

'Our village lay in the heart of perhaps the strictest preserved county in England at that day. It was a pretty little village enough: the forest came up within a mile of it on one side while an inclosed, rich agricultural country stretched for miles around on the other. The forest land was full of pheasants, hares and rabbits while the open country swarmed with partridges.

'The whole district for miles around belonged to the Duke of B., one of our strictest game preservers while his head keeper Johnson was the very type of his calling, a stout, heavy, muscular, middle-aged man, able-bodied and resolute. He was the terror of all poachers round us for he looked on them as the rankest of vermin and if he could have had his own way he would have hung them from the branches of his keeper's "tree" with as little remorse as polecats or weasels.

'Our village was a nest of poachers and Johnson used to reckon that on any night we could turn out a gang of half a score of the most determined poachers in the county, men well versed in the minutiae of their trade who could snare a hare in an open furrow as well as a smeuse, who could silently sweep off covey after covey of birds in a night in the very heart of the manor; who could clear the home preserves close up to the keepers lodge without firing a shot but who could at times muster in a gang armed with guns and, laying aside all secrecy, march through the forest and nail the pheasants at perch like so many barn door fowls.

'Every one of those poachers was a marked man and every one in the village knew well how we obtained a livelihood during the Winter months but they were always civil and respectful enough to us and somehow or other none of us who had no game to preserve seemed to think that poaching was a grave offence.

'Of course there was a leader of this gang and he was a man in every respect fitted for his post. He was the son of an old higgler and a more ruffianly fellow it would have been hard to find. His name was Bill Hammerton and was known all over the county by the nickname 'Sloppy'. He was at this time a little over thirty years, a stout, thickset fellow standing about 5 feet 9 inches and weighing 13 stone. A more desperate character did not exist and unless rumour grossly lied, far darker charges than poaching could be laid at his door.

'Although he had been imprisoned three or four times for snaring, he had always been lucky enough to escape being taken in any night affray. This was the more singular, for he was always at the head of his gang and in the thickest of the fray in the night encounters which then were taking place so frequently between poachers and gamekeepers. He was a noted fighter and champion of the county. Scarcely a village feast or country fair for miles around but this Bill Hammerton was engaged in a pugilistic contest.

'Johnson was himself as brave as a lion and would have given any money to capture Hammerton in a night row for a price was set upon his head and if he was taken, the gang would in all probability be broken up. But he had never yet been lucky enough.

'One night there had been a desperate battle in the woods not two miles from us and I recollect well that I sat on our garden wall and counted nearly one hundred shots fired about eleven o' clock before the keepers came up. The battle was a sharp one but the keepers as usual got the best of it. Three poachers were taken, the rest escaped including our groom who was among them. His hat had been knocked off in the melée and the keeper secured it. He read the man's name in it and next morning rode over to see if we could identify it. It was no trouble to do this. The man never came back to us and neither did we hear of him again . . .

'There was something cheery in the light of the blacksmith's forge as I approached the village so I dismounted. As I looked through the open door I saw the shop was full as usual and I recognised four of five poachers I knew well. One was just unscrewing a short gun barrel which he thrust into his pocket as I drew up. He was followed by a little half-starved lurcher cur which never left his heels and which, as a mute dog for driving hares into the nets, was invaluable to the gang.

'As I got off my horse he asked me in a low tone if I wanted a hare or a brace of longtails in the morning. I told him they had better look out, for Johnson was expecting

them. He laughed and said "they knew it, but they wanted game that night and game they would have". This was the last conversation I ever had with that poor fellow for he was dead by morning. Of course Bill Hammerton was in the shop, apparently engaged in heating some wire at the blacksmith's forge, no doubt for snares.

'It was a curious thing but whenever any great poaching visit was planned to a favourite preserve, our keepers always seemed to know of it beforehand and be prepared. In fact sometimes out of sheer bravado the poachers would send word to say that they were coming on such a night and hoped the keepers would meet them like men.

'Now on this night there was to be a grand "gathering" of the clans to sweep the home preserves before the Christmas battues began. Four gangs from four different villages had agreed to meet at the old trysting place, a gravel pit by the side of the forest. Twenty of the best men were to be told off to shoot the pheasants in the home woods and the rest were to quickly net the hares and rabbits in the forest. The poachers reckoned that they should muster about thirty-five men, which they did. As I said before, Johnson was prepared for them but with all his watchers he could not reckon on more than eight men so he applied for help from the head keeper whose preserves he joined.

'On this estate every labourer was obliged to take his turn at night watching, so he had no difficulty in borrowing twelve men for this occasion. This was common sense to the keepers for if the poachers had swept our woods first they would certainly have gone to the other estate on another night. The neighbouring head keeper agreed to head them just for the fun of the thing. Johnson's men were never allowed any other weapons except sticks, each had a handkerchief tied round his head to distinguish him, a rather useful precaution in a night affray where the rule was, if you see a head, hit it. Johnson himself had a most singular weapon, a stout hayfork about three feet long in the shaft, "a tolloch over the had with that, (I use his own expressive phrase), would bring the strongest man to his knees like a bullock". I saw this identical hayfork at his house a few days after the battle and the tines were bent crooked over Bill Hammerton's head.

'The keepers of the Duke of B. always fought with short dog spears. On the night the keepers mustered about twenty, the poachers about thirty-five men. These seemed long odds, but still they were in favour of the keepers for "thrice armed is he who has his quarrel just". Besides, as Johnson observed to me, "Bless you! When you come to tackle a poacher, he's very little good. He's never got anything in him but gin and tobacco. They don't get a good meal of meat but once a week", which I dare say was about true.

'By ten the poachers had mustered in the gravel pit by the side of a lane, close to the forest where the netting was to commence. The keepers, who were not up to their trick of dividing, went down to one of the home preserves nearly a mile from the gravel pit where they fancied the general attack would be made. But they went to the wrong spot, for they waited for nearly half an hour without hearing a sound and they almost began to think that the poachers had abandoned any idea of coming that night when a double shot was fired in the wood close to the village, more than a mile from where they were watching.

'This shot was fired about half-past ten and I was standing in the stable yard talking with Jem. We both heard it and he observed, "That's only a plant to draw the keepers down; it's not that wood they mean to work tonight". In a little time we counted five more shots and then all was still. I may add that it was the night above all others that the poachers love. I never could imagine that the man who wrote the old poaching song of "My delight on a shiny night . . ." knew much about real poaching as our chaps never went out at the full moon for a great attack. A dark, gusty, blowing night with the moon certainly not older than ten days was the night they generally chose. Tonight the wind was blowing fresh from the South West so that the reports of the guns were carried plain enough to our village which lay to leeward of the wood, but the keepers who were upwind never heard them so that the ruse, although well planned, entirely failed.

'At about eleven, however, the general attack began. I may add that Hammerton was to head the shooting party and the young man I had spoken to in the blacksmith's shop headed the netters. The poachers had gone to a home preserve full of pheasants which were perching low on account of the storm. This wood lay rather to windward of the keepers so they heard the shots but only indistinctly, soon five of them to the minute all over the wood.

' "By God!" said Johnson, "They're in the home wood. Come on my lads or they'll clear it before we get there." And off the keepers started in the direction of the guns. But the road was rough and the moon gave little light. It was not easy running and it was half an hour before they reached the wood. After the first twenty minutes the fire slackened and in the time they got up, the poachers were beating a retreat to join their companions who were netting in another covert about half a mile distant. It was excellently planned. Hammerton got all his men off but three who lay hidden with game in a ditch by the very side of which the keepers passed in hot pursuit without discovering them. It was unlucky for Johnson that his favourite night dog (Old Sailor) had staked himself the day before in jumping over a dead fence with a pheasant in his mouth and was obliged to be left at home for these men and their booty would have been secured. As it was they lay quiet till the keepers had passed and then ran home as fast as they could under a load of about

fifty of Johnson's finest pheasants which had cost nearly £1 each to fatten. By five in the morning they were on top of one of the night coaches and the same night were in London.

'It had been planned beforehand that directly the firing ceased the poachers who were netting were to assemble under a large oak well known to every one of them and wait till the Hammerton party joined them. He rightly guessed that the keepers would come down in a body to the guns and if they could only get a quarter of an hour's good shooting he would leave off and retreat quickly to the netting party so that in case of attack their forces would not be divided.

'The old oak was perhaps five hundred yards in the depth of the forest and as the poachers stood as mute and silent as statues beneath its shades the keepers were completely at fault. Had the poachers been content to carry with them a part of the hares and rabbits which they had secured and silently retreated they would have got clear off, but they wished to save their nets which were worth ten or fifteen pounds so they stood still, thinking that the keepers might overlook them in the gloom.

'The keepers were standing consulting in the thick wood within two hundred yards of the tree little thinking how close they were to the poachers. They were about to turn back when suddenly the clouds lifted and the moon shone out in all her glory. Those few minutes enabled the keepers to see the poachers and Johnson's shout of triumph, "Here they are! Close in, my lads!" warned them that there was nothing for it but stand up and fight like men. All their faces were blackened and many of them disfigured with red patches and they formed a wild group when their uncouth figures and the old dead tree were suddenly brought into bold relief by the moon.

'The keepers dashed into the open space but the poachers presented a formidable front, for those who had guns were ranged in line, every muzzle presented to them. They drew back and hesitated and Johnson's challenge of "Come, my men, no nonsense! We know you all so you'd better give up!" was met with a derisive jeer from the poachers who bade them come in if they dared.

'Johnson's blood was up. He had recognised his old enemy Hammerton in the crowd and was determined to have him or die in the attempt. Heedless of all consequences he rushed at him, and the keepers, instead of showing a front line, followed him in Indian file and the attack was so sudden that only two guns were fired, one charge wounding a keeper in the thigh. "No firing! Butt ends, my lads!" roared out Hammerton as he sprung aside and aimed a heavy blow at Johnson's head with the butt end of his gun, but the hayfork stood the keeper in good stead for he parried the blow which would probably have dashed out his brains, and recovering he brought Hammerton to the ground with a swinging round-handed hit on the side of the head.

'The poacher fell and the keeper who was overbalanced by the force of his own blow fell on him. Hammerton was not even stunned and he seized Johnson like a bulldog by the throat and these two strong men rolled over and over on the grass in a mortal embrace, snarling and tearing at each other like two fierce dogs sometimes one above, sometimes the other.

'Meanwhile the battle was raging fiercely all around, now and then a crashing blow from a gunstock would bring a keeper to the ground, but the short dog spears did dreadful service. The men were ordered to use them as sticks and not stab with them but more than one poacher fell with a dog spear in his side. In the whole battle only three guns were fired but this is accounted for by the fact that only five of the poachers had any ammunition left and had the keepers but known that only five of the twenty guns which were pointed at them were loaded they would not have hesitated about rushing in.

'The battle was too fierce to last long and in five minutes the poachers beat a retreat leaving seven prisoners and all their nets, hares and rabbits in the hands of the keepers. Poor Johnson was in an awkward case. He could not rise for he could not shake Hammerton off who was as strong as himself. By a desperate struggle the poacher got above the keeper and dashing his head to the ground which partially stunned him, he sprang to his feet and giving Johnson one settler by a tremendous kick under the ear, he plunged into the thickest of the forest and, favoured by the confusion of the moment, escaped.

'It was some time before Johnson could rise and his first expression as he stared wildly around him; "Damn him, I'll have him yet", proved how sorry he felt for the loss of his prize which he considered fairly in his grasp. Several of the keepers had broken heads but none was seriously hurt except the man who was shot in the thigh and one of the young watchers who gave chase to a poacher for some hundreds of yards into the forest. The poacher finding himself sorely pressed suddenly threw himself down, the watcher tumbled over him and, before he could rise, was stunned by a blow from the poacher's bludgeon who then made his escape. The prisoners, with their booty, were marched off to Johnson's lodge and next morning were taken before a neighbouring magistrate and committed for trial at the next assizes.

'When the keepers mustered, one was missing, the young watcher who had followed the poacher into the wood. In vain did his comrades shout, in vain did their shrill whistles sound through the wood. In the end they left the wood without him. In the morning he staggered up to the keeper's cottage pale as death, sick and faint, his head and face covered with blood and wearing such a ghastly appearance that the other keepers hardly knew him.

'The poacher had left him stunned and disabled and it was a long time before he came to himself. He tried to find his way home as best he could and his instincts soon put him on the right path and partly by walking and partly by crawling on all fours he managed to find his way to the edge of the covert. The night was not black as pitch for the moon had gone down.

'He was staggering along a narrow ride in the forest when his foot struck against something that lay in his path and he stumbled over the dead body of the young poacher who had headed the netting party. He had been stabbed in the side with a dog spear but had run as far as his strength could carry him till he fell dead from internal bleeding. His poor little dog kept watch over his body and was endeavouring to lick his hands and face and pulled at his coat to awake his dead master, but in vain.

'The poor fellow was buried in our churchyard and of all the mourners that followed him to the grave, not one deplored his loss more deeply than that ragged little half-starved cur. The keeper fell over the dead body and for some time lay at the side of the corpse. He was already faint with pain and loss of blood and when his hand came into contact with that cold face and dabbled in the blood which surrounded the dead poacher it was more than he could stand: he fainted dead away.

'The night breeze swept in ghostly gusts through the dead trees and the dismal hoot of the owl echoed mournfully through the forest glade but the two sleepers heard nothing. It was not until daylight glimmered in the east that the watcher awoke and the grey twilight of a drear Winter's morning revealed to him the ghastly features of the dead man

who had been his companion through the night upon the damp, chill bed on which they had both fallen.

'The poacher's death caused no little sensation among our simple villagers and a sad ballad was made by some rustic poet about that fateful night; it was a standard song at harvest homes for years to come:

> The keepers heard us fire a gun,
> And to the spot did quickly run,
> And swore before the rising sun
> That one of us should die.

'The poachers were tried at the next assizes, but their sentence was not so heavy as we expected. The incident of the poacher killed by the dog spear influenced judge and jury. The gang was broken up and although poaching was carried on on a small scale, we rarely heard afterwards of any serious battles in our woods which, before that night, were so constantly taking place between keepers and poachers.

'Hammerton escaped the vigilance of the police for two years notwithstanding a reward offered for his apprehension and he was a well known character in our parts.'

Two cameos stand out for me in this lively account: one is of the wild poachers led by the ferocious Hammerton, their faces daubed with red and black waiting in dead silence and stone still under the great oak tree, watchful and ready for action. The other is of the two lads lying together, one dead, the other as dead, while the little dog licked at the face of his master.

'All the pheasants ever bred, won't repay for one man dead.'

· THE END OF THE BLACKGUARD · HAMMERTON

The notorious Hammerton who was involved with the great affray described so vividly by the 'Old Bushman' was not done yet. His cry of 'No firing lads! Use your butt ends!' went in his favour at his trial so he was sent to prison for two years when he might have expected a heavier sentence. He 'did his time' and returned to his old village harbouring a deep grudge against Johnson his old adversary who had been responsible for his two years' 'hard'. He was thirsting for revenge.

'. . . one afternoon as Johnson was riding home from the village he met his old enemy walking into it, returning after his term in prison. Hammerton politely bade the keeper "Good afternoon", thanked him for his "kindness" and told him he would never forget it, words uttered by as great a ruffian as ever breathed. Johnson was not a man to be frightened by words and telling the poacher that he had better not let him get hold of him again he rode on. Hammerton certainly had not forgotten Johnson's "kindness" but took an early opportunity of repaying the obligation.

'It was soon evident that Hammerton was organising another gang for Winter, for while many of his old gang had settled down as steady labourers, there were still a few lawless spirits who were too far gone ever to reform. Johnson doubled his team of night watchers and there would have been rough work that Winter if Hammerton could have kept himself quiet through the Summer, but he was longing to be revenged upon Johnson and could not wait. It was not easy, as Johnson rarely went out without a gun and Old Sailor never left his heels and was as good and better than any man.

'Johnson left the village feast; he had neither dog nor gun with him. On his road home half way between our village and his lodge was a small spinney and just as he passed a double shot came from that direction. He tied his pony to the gate and ran down the ditch under cover of the hedge to see what was up and when he reached the coppice a well-dressed man, a stranger, was standing loading his gun about twenty yards into the wood.

'The man made no attempt to escape and his response to Johnson's challenge, "Who the Devil are you?" was, "You'd better come and see". Johnson was scrambling over the hedge into the spinney when suddenly another man sprang up from the ditch behind him where he had been covered in a heap of ferns and in less time than it takes to write it, the keeper was knocked senseless into the ditch by a blow on the back of the head from a gun stock; in those few seconds Johnson had time to recognise the brutal features of Hammerton.

'Their strategem had worked well for they had watched Johnson leave the feast and laid a trap. Murder most assuredly have been added to the list of Hammerton's iniquities but as luck would have it, three farm labourers came over the hedge at the end of the copse at the very minute that Hammerton was standing over the fallen man, his gun raised ready to give the coup de grace. A sharp exclamation from the man in the wood caused him to turn round and he saw the three labourers not fifty yards from him. His second blow fell harmlessly and he dashed away at once through the spinney and made his escape with his comrade on the other side of it. The labourers had seen him, but dared not follow and turned their attention to the apparently lifeless keeper.

'The youngest of the three ran down to the village on the keeper's pony to tell the news, the other two carried the body to the road, and in less than half an hour Johnson's brother drove up in a tax cart and took him to his lodge. Although his skull was dreadfully fractured he was not dead. Brain fever set in and for weeks his life hung upon a thread. A strong constitution, however, pulled him through and although he was never the same man again, he still kept his place as head keeper but under strict injunctions that he never again went out to watch at night.

'It was not likely that such a desperate attack in broad daylight should pass unnoticed. A hundred pounds reward was now offered by Johnson's master for Hammerton's apprehension and as a good London detective was set on his trail he did not long escape. He was apprehended in London, tried at our next Assizes and sentence of death passed upon him. The other man was never taken and Hammerton's sullen remark that he "would never split upon a pal with the halter round his neck" gave the police very little hopes of ever obtaining information from him.

'Hammerton was transported for life, and after serving in a convict gang for some years he obtained a ticket of leave and when the diggings first broke out, like many others of his stamp, had an extraordinary run of luck. But his eyesight failed him and he set up a weather-board lodging house and sly grog shop on Forest Creek.

'This hairy, purblind old ruffian to look at, whose brutal countenance tempts you to ask "Could such a man ever have been a baby?", complete with "overseer's brand", (a broken nose), whose chief delight was to growl out his deeds of villainy in his peculiar colonial slang, smoked his short pipe in the evenings round the fire. I have sat and listened scores of times to his conversation but I do not believe that ever in a single instance did I hear the man utter a sentence of regret for his past life.'

Thus was the end of the fearful Hammerton, and it is intriguing to reflect that there are well-to-do families living in Australia today, in the greatest of respectability and even affluence, who have smart cars, good homes and who happily go surfing, who are direct descendants of that most terrible poacher and blackguard, the likes of whom was mirrored in other villages of his time, but who cast a black shadow over his little community all the time he was there.

· A POACHER'S DISGUISE ·

The new keeper is determined to clear the parish of poachers and this leads to a nasty incident; this tale was told me by a man who was a child at the time of the affair.

'It was said that the shooting took place one early morning. The two of them were shooting birds when they were come upon by Keeper Jenkins and his undermen. These two poachers were outnumbered; had they not been, it is doubtful if two men could have been found to face them – let alone apprehend them.

'The two wore what was then known as a "havelock". It was a covering for the whole of the head and shoulders excepting two eye holes through which the wearer could see. Even the slit through which the poacher could breathe was covered with thin muslin. In addition to this weird head-dress they wore a smock complete with a kilt which fell well below the knee. The necessity for this disguise emphasises the sternness of the whole business. Detection was to be avoided at all costs as punishments were terribly drastic, the days of transportation being not long gone. Thus poachers could not be recognised and the only way to apprehend them was to take them in the act, even if it meant battle.

'At dawn the new keeper made a fair catch, as the poachers were weighted down with birds, guns and nets; they could not escape by fleetness of foot and the keepers had equal knowledge of the countryside. Keeper Jenkins was warned to stand back or take the consequences. As to whether he was a brave man or thought the poachers would not shoot, I do not know. One thing is certain, they were not evenly matched.

'One poacher shot in the direction of Jenkins and it is possible he was 'sprinted' with a few pellets. What the poachers expected happened and the keepers took to their heels. What would have happened had the keepers not run I cannot say, but the poachers were more determined in spite of the fact that the keepers also had guns.

'An arrest was made later, the keeper swearing he had recognised the man who fired the shot. In court he stuck to his story, until the defending lawyer asked the bench for permission to leave the court for a few moments. When he returned he was wearing a full havelock and kilt as worn by the poachers on that fateful night. "Your Worship, even my own mother would not recognise me in such a garb."

'The witness was rebuked by the judge as a liar and perjuror, and he added "If I could, I would put you in prison where this poor man had been for so long".'

· A KEEPER IS BESTED ·

This is a tale sent to me by the retired Norfolk keeper Dick Townsend, recounting the time he had a nasty encounter with poachers reminiscent of the worst of the old Victorian days of violence, and one in which he is bested by one with the blood of Bill Hammerton in his veins. The keepers did not always get it their own way, and Dick tells this story against himself in a matter of fact way which is both appealing and philosophical.

'When I first took on the situation at Scottow I was warned by my employer that there was part of the estate which was more or less left to itself. This was known locally as "Poachers' Paradise". The old retired head keeper who I had replaced also told me to watch out over there, for there were two or three rough gangs regularly poaching that ground; it was a haven for them.

'It had two disused roads running through it which had been closed when the airfield was built, as well as two bridlepaths and a footpath that went along the side of one of the woods. People had the right to use any of these roads and paths and could not be challenged by a keeper, which was very frustrating. You had to be very lucky indeed to catch someone who had shot a bird before he got to one of those safe rights of way.

'Before I had my night of bad luck I had a bit of good luck. I was standing in a deep ditch hoping I might get a shot at a pigeon when a covey of eleven partridges flew over the hedge from behind and settled no more than 15 to 20 yards in front of me. I knew they had been disturbed, by the way they behaved, and decided to keep still and watch them. Several minutes later there was a hell of a bang after which a man jumped over the bank about three yards to my right to gather his kill. He was too late, for I was ready for him and made sure he was not going to get away. I also knew he was not much of a poacher for if he had known his job, most probably he could have shot the lot of them without any flying away. I tell this story as I am almost positive it had some bearing on the tale I am about to tell.

'It was a very windy and rough night, not over dark, but it would be lighter later on when the moon got up so I decided to go for a drink and chat with my mates for an hour. I left the pub at about 10.30 and decided to drive to Poachers' Paradise and listen to any sounds that might tell me someone was about.

'I had been hanging on for over an hour and heard nothing, and feeling chilly I decided to walk over to my other wood to warm myself up. Just before the wood was a concrete platform which the farmer used for loading sugar beet and also a big heap of beet. As I walked to the wood I saw a car parked behind the beet and felt sure it had no right to be there. I couldn't take the number as it was too dark and naturally there were no lights on. I thought perhaps it might be a courting couple and decided that as they were on private ground, I would ask them to leave and in this way find out the car number at the same time.

'As I went across to the car I could see two people sitting in the front and when I got near it the one in the driver's seat opened his door and said. "What are you after?" I said, "I've come to see what this car is doing on private land." His reply was, "Well, what are you going to do about it?" I just managed to say, "I'm going to ask you to move off . . ." when I felt a crashing blow from behind which knocked me down forwards onto my knees.

'I was about to get up when another blow, which I felt sure was from someone's boot, caught me full force in the left eye. I still wasn't going to give in and tried to get up but they made damn sure I wouldn't by giving me a beauty in the stomach which completely winded me. I realised the one who landed the first blow must have been hiding behind the car.

'Anyway, they were soon gone, with no lights on and even if there had been I was in no state to take the number. I sat on the beet heap for a while until I had got my breath back, then made my way back to my car.

'It was 2.30am when I got home and looked in the mirror – it was not a pretty sight! Still, I reflected, I'd been lucky through the years and you can't win 'em all!'

· A VIOLENT ENCOUNTER ·

Thomas Turner at the turn of the century confronts a poaching gang which stands in a row, backs to the fence ready to fight, looking strange and fierce in their long, bulky coats, the mist swirling round them in the moonlight. This extract is also taken from Memoirs of a Gamekeeper.

'I said, "You are fairly caught, chaps; no nonsense." However, they did not offer to give themselves up but stood with sticks raised. I went up to a man on the right, hit him and dragged him out of the line. I handed him over to an elderly keeper and said, "Hold him, John". I went up to the next man, collared him by the neckerchief and attempted to repeat the performance. This man said, "It's not coming off like that", and the fight began.

'He lost his cudgel but took my pick-shaft away from me so I closed and wrestled it back. In the meantime there was general fight. They set the dogs on us so I had to kick the dogs off behind whilst I fought the man in front. Eventually I struck his right arm muscle but still he declared, "I won't go with you". I said, "I will have you, alive or dead", for my blood was up and finally he had to surrender.

'I am sorry to say that two of our men showed the white feather, leaving four of us to fight six of them. We held fast to the two men we had taken, and the four who escaped were later identified. The six poachers were all convicted to terms of imprisonment with hard labour because they had used violence. The man who had given me such a tussle was the leader of the gang and a famous fighting man. The poaching fraternity never recovered from this setback and the gangs ceased to visit the estate.

'After we had given evidence in court a young keeper and myself were waiting in the lobby in case we should be wanted again; two young toughs came in and began to insult us. We could do little about it. A young policeman ordered them to behave themselves. They refused, and the constable promptly threw one of them down the stairs into the street. The second one did not wait for similar treatment.'

· A POACHER'S DOGS TURN THE TABLES ·

John Connell writing in Confessions of a Poacher in 1901 tells of a poacher attacked by two keepers. They had lured the poacher towards them by a ruse by which they pretended to be his companions, who were in fact elsewhere at the time catching hares. The poacher was prepared to surrender, but when attacked by the two men was saved severe punishment thanks to his trusty lurcher, Nellie, backed up by the formidable Blucher, a greyhound-cross-bulldog crossed with a German boarhound, a truly fearful monster.

'Suddenly I found myself seized from behind by the younger man who punched the back of my head and shook me violently. His grip was like a vice and I began to feel that I was securely trapped. All at once I saw that the man in front was being attacked by my dog Nellie; he hit her two or three times with a stick, but without a sound she flew at him again and again and compelled him to retreat rapidly. The man behind still shook and punched me as if to inspire me with terror. I tried to turn round, but could not. But at this moment he emitted an "Ugh!" which was obviously the result of pain and to my surprise, loosed his hold.

'Turning towards him I saw with delight that he was being attacked by Blucher. This eased my mind as I knew from experienced that anyone whom Blucher fought would get all he deserved and perhaps more, and this man carried a much lighter stick than the other so I turned my back on him.

'I found that the shorter man had been driven back some twelve or fifteen yards by Nellie and he was vigorously endeavouring to defend himself from her teeth by kicks and blows which seldom found their mark. Fearing that he might kill her with a heavy blow on the head, I ran forward and without striking him, parried the blows with my stick.

'Her severe attentions to his legs made him execute a step-dance better than many stage performances that I have paid money to watch. I soon saw that he was appealing, "Call her off!" – never did the fortunes of war change more quickly.

'By this time I could hear the man behind me emit alternate oaths and yells. I was in no hurry to call Nellie off; my would-be captor had not yet surrendered and I wanted a clear understanding with him before agreeing to an armistice.

'At length he called out, "Are you a man at all?" Then I stopped her. He next wanted to go to the assistance of his companion but I barred that. For a couple of minutes we watched the fight between Blucher and his enemy which was becoming a very one-sided affair. The keeper was getting exhausted and Blucher was just warming to his work. He was a very big dog, weighing ninety-six pounds and, like all his kind, was as active as a cat. A bite from him was dangerous.

'At first he fought cautiously, retreating instantly after each bite and contending himself mainly with tearing the man's clothes. The fellow was in tatters and the bites were beginning to tell. The keeper fought like a Trojan. His stick was smashed to atoms and his cuffs and kicks were quite unavailing. He began to emit piteous yells and the other one bawled at me, "Do you want to see the man killed?" Indeed, I began to fear that his life was in danger. But I was confronted with the problem of how to get Blucher off.

'To call him was not the slightest use, because when his blood was up he would not obey me. To strike him was equally useless; he took no notice of the blows. I knew he must be pulled off by main strength, but in this line I had had a very unpleasant experience: on a former occasion in the middle of an encounter I had tried to pull him off by one of his hind legs, but turning round like lightning he had made his fangs almost meet through my arm. Of course the poor fellow did not know whom he was biting in the excitement of the moment.

'I now shouted his name two or three times to recall to him a sense of my presence and, seizing a favourable moment, threw myself on him, clasped him round the body and held him. Luckily he did not bite me. He struggled to get at the keeper again, but finding I held him fast soon became quieter. I drew from my pocket a leather collar which I buckled on his neck, and took a firm grip.

'The older man called out to his companion, "Bill, are you very much bitten?" The answer came at once, "___ me, I'm bitten all over!" I remarked sincerely that I was sorry for what had occurred. I pointed out that if they had allowed me to go quietly at first no one would have been a penny worse; and then I made for the road. All this time I kept a firm grip on Blucher's collar as I knew from experience that if I loosed him he would go back and attack the man again. I soon reached the road and walked briskly in the direction in which I expected to meet my friends.'

The two keepers followed our hero up the lane but he threatened them that if they came with him another yard he would loose Blucher. This had the effect of stopping them in their tracks. The poacher made good his escape by train to London, and after two weeks under a surgeon, the young keeper made a full recovery.

· A ROUGH GANG IS TAKEN ·

In Memoirs of a Gamekeeper *we read that in 1893 Mr Turner, the noted Elvedon gamekeeper, was a youngster of twenty-five. Those were the hard times of serious poaching affrays and desperate men. Alone and at night he had once approached a rough gang of poachers, but these, seeing that he was a youngster and on his own, had threatened him with murder and wisely he had run away with the whole gang after him. However, the following December at Ash Plantation on the High Lodge Farm he was to meet them again – but this time he was not alone.*

'The time was 10.30pm. It was a beautiful bright moonlight night with a rustling breeze, ideal conditions for poaching. This time we were seven in number and we waited in the shadows. The wire fence in front of us was laid down to enable us to make a rush if necessary. Would they come? Hark, something was astir in the direction of Cooksey Hill opposite our position. Two dogs trotted past but made no sign of alarm. I confess I was trembling with excitement. Then the poachers, five in number, came unsuspectingly towards us – and this time I was not alone!

'When they were quite near, our second keeper said. "You have come the wrong night, my lads!" The poachers immediately fell into line facing us and said, "Come on, you ___!" We made a rush and the fight was soon over. One man bolted but Fred Reeve, one of our number, gave chase and brought him back.

'We took the gang to a farmhouse at High Lodge where they were given some beer to drink. One of their number had come into contact with a big cudgel and he looked to be in sorry condition indeed. No one else was seriously hurt on either side. I had lost the top of a knuckle trying to guard the top of my head, but this did not matter for we had at last captured our first gang of Isleham poachers who had knocked keepers about and terrorised the countryside for years. One of them was a ruffian who had been in jail for assaults and violence.

'We took the poachers in two horses and traps to Mildenhall Police Station where they were duly locked up. Later they received sentences varying from two to three months with hard labour.

'When the case was tried, all the poaching fraternity came to Mildenhall to show their support for the accused. They were a very rough lot indeed. After the hearing the gamekeepers went into a hotel for lunch. The poachers' dogs, which had been detained by the police, had been handed back to the poachers' friends to be taken home: the crowd now brought these dogs to the front of the hotel and challenged us to go out and take them again. The challenge was not accepted.

'The seven members of our party were afterwards each presented with a silver-mounted walking stick, duly inscribed, in recognition of the success. The presentation was made by the trustees of the Elvedon estate.'

· A NASTY INCIDENT ·

The history of game preservation is peppered with fights in woodlands at night and there are many recorded examples, some told from the keeper's, some from the poacher's point of view. This story, written by an anonymous poacher who operated in the final two decades of Victoria's reign, is a good example; it also indicates that the 'lads' in those days were a fairly tough bunch.

'One night in November when the trees were bare and the pheasants had taken to the branches, we were in a mixed wood of pine and beech. A good many birds roosted in its confines and, to a practised eye, were not difficult to see against the moon as they sat on the lower limbs of the trees near the trunks. I and my companion had old, strong guns with barrels filed down and as we got very near the birds, we were using small charges of powder. As the night was windy the shots would not be heard very far off and we felt fairly safe. When we had obtained about three brace of birds, however, I heard a sudden crashing among the underwood, when I immediately sprung behind the trunk of a tree and kept closely against it.

'The head keeper had my companion down before he could resist, and I only remained undiscovered for a few seconds. One of the underkeepers seized me, but being a good wrestler, I soon threw him into a dense brake of brambles and blackthorn. Then I bolted with the third man close behind. I could easily have outrun him over the rough country that lay outside the wood, but there was a stiff stone fence fully five feet high betwixt me and the open: unless I could "fly" the fence he would have me.

'I clutched my pockets, steadied myself for the leap and then sprang. I heard my pursuer stop for a second to await the issue. Weighted as I was, I caught the coping and fell back heavily into the wood. As soon as the keeper saw I was down he rushed forward and hit me heavily on the head with a stave. The sharp edge cut right through to the bone and the blood spurted out in little jets. Then I turned about, determined to close with my opponent if he was inclined for further roughness – but he was not. When he saw that the blood was almost blinding me, he dropped his hedge stake and ran, apparently terrified at what he had done.

'I leaned for a few moments on the wall, then dragged myself over and started for a stream that ran down the field. But I felt weaker at every step, and soon crept into a bed of tall brackens and plugged the wound in my head with a handful of wet moss, keeping it in position with my neckerchief. After this I munched on some bread and hard cheese, sucked the dew from the fern fronds and then fell into a broken sleep.

'I must have slept for four or five hours, when I awoke thirsty and feverish and very weak. I tried to walk, but again and again fell down. Then I crawled for about a hundred yards, but this caused my wound to bleed afresh and I fainted. Just as day was coming, a farm labourer came across and kindly helped me to his cottage. He and his wife bathed my head and eyes and assisted me to the bed from which they had just risen. At noon I was able to take some bread and milk, and at night, an hour after darkness had fallen, I was able to start for home.'

In the subsequent court case the keeper claimed 'self-defence', but in the end the charge was dropped by a magistrate who felt sympathy for the poacher's wounds. The author's companion was less fortunate: he got 'two months hard'!

· A BLOODY AFFRAY WITH · DEER POACHERS

Deer poachers in Wiltshire came armed with corn flails in this eighteenth-century tale of alarum and bloody affray. They engaged in a pitched battle with the keepers which, in keeping with the general pattern of such things, led to the inevitable injuries and in this case an amputation. This account is by the Rev W. Chafin, written in 1818 and appears in Anecdotes of Cranbourne Chase.

'On the night of 16th December 1780, a very severe battle was fought between the keepers and deer stealers on Chettle Common in Bursey-stool-Walk which was attended with very serious circumstances. A gang of these deer stealers assembled at Pimperne and were headed by a Sergeant of Dragoons, a native of Pimperne and then quartered at Blandford, whose name was Blandford. They came in the night in disguise armed with deadly and offensive weapons called Swindgels, resembling flails to thresh corn.

'They attacked the keepers who were nearly equal in number, but had no weapons but sticks and short hangers. The first blow that was struck was by the leader of the gang which broke the kneecap of the stoutest man in the Chase, who was not only disabled from joining the combat but who has been lame ever since. Another keeper received a blow from a swindgel which broke three ribs and was the cause of his death some time after.

'The remaining keepers closed in upon their opponents with their hangers, and one of the Dragoon's hands was severed from the arm just above the wrist and fell to the ground; the others also were dreadfully cut and wounded and were obliged to surrender. Blandford's arm was tightly bound with a list garter to prevent its bleeding and he was carried to the lodge where I saw him the next day and his hand in the window. Peter Beckford Esq, who was at that time Ranger of the Walk, came early in the morning and brought Mr. Dansey, a very eminent surgeon with him who dressed the wound and administered proper remedies to the poor patient. Two young officers came also in the course of the day to see him.

'As soon as he was well enough to be removed, he was committed with his companions to Dorchester gaol. The hand was buried in Pimperne churchyard and, as reported, with the honours of war. Several of the offenders were labourers, daily employed by Mr. Beckford and had, the preceding day, dined in his servants' hall and from thence went to join a confederacy to rob their master.

'They were all tried by Sir Richard Perryn at the Dorchester Assizes, found guilty and condemned to be transported for seven years but, in consideration of their great suffering from their wounds in prison, the humane judge commuted the punishment to confinement in gaol for an indefinite term. The soldier was not dismissed from His Majesty's Service but suffered to retire on half pay or pension and set up as a game factor in London . . . The person who cut off his arm is alive and well.'

EPILOGUE

An Old Poacher reflects on mortality . . .

The children are scattered
The old folks now gone.
Why stand I here like a ghost in the meadow?
It's time I was passing
It's time I passed on.

Traditional

ACKNOWLEDGEMENTS

This book would have been impossible without the help of many people. There were those who sent reminiscences or yarns from their family and friends, some of whom preferred to maintain a discreet anonymity. Some sent old books, crumbled newspaper cuttings and old magazines. Many publishers and authors were kind in allowing me to use material from their work. Honest attempts have been made to contact all source providers and if any have slipped through the net I apologise and will be happy to make amends as best I can.

Individuals who were especially kind were:

Chippy Smith of Devon, an old-timer and part-time keeper.
Dick Townsend, a retired Norfolk keeper who sent me many wonderful and well written tales.
Gil Gaylor who helped with *Poachers' Tales* and who sent me his account of the Fox twins.
Mark Lorne of Norfolk for his yarns about the remarkable 'Lijah.
David Grayling of Crosby in Cumbria, the antiquarian book collector and dealer who sent me some ancient stories which were invaluable.
Many anonymous folk who helped as they saw fit.

Extracts have also been quoted from the following:
Anon. *The Sportsman's Dictionary*
Bell, W.D.M. 'The Wanderings of an Elephant Hunter', *Country Life* (1923)
Blome, Richard. *Gentleman's Recreation* (1686)
Connell, John. *Confessions of a Poacher* (London, 1901)
Dewar, George. *The Faery Year* (1906)
Fawcett, Richard. *Pennine Poacher* (Dalesman Books, 1984)
Fitzgerald, Brian Vesey. *It's my Delight* (Eyre and Spottiswoode, 1947)
Fur, Feather and Fin, Volume One, 'The Pheasant' (Longman, 1895)
Hanger, Col George. *To all Sportsmen* (1814)
Jefferies, Richard. *The Amateur Poacher* (Oxford, 1879)
Jeffrey, Sir Peter. *The Keepers Book* (Lonsdale Library)
Open Field magazine
St John, Charles. *A Tour of Sutherland* (London, 1849)
St John, Charles. *Wild Sports and Natural History of the Highlands* (London, 1893)
Scrope, William. *Days of Deerstalking* (Edward Arnold, 1897)
Stonehenge. *British Rural Sports* (Routledge, 1856)
The Old Bushman. *Sporting Sketches at Home and Abroad* (1866)
The Shooting Times (1950)
Willock, Colin. *Kenzie the Wild Goose Man* (Deutsch, 1962)
Wyman, Harold. *The Great Game* (Fieldfare Books, 1990)

INDEX

INDEX

Snares/snaring, 16, 45-6, 58, 61-4, 67, 76, 79, 94, 95, 98-9, 103, 111, 119, 127, 135, 138, 154
Snipe, 20, 111, 127
Snow, 41, 46, 76, 107
Spears, 11; dog, 158, 160, 161, 163; falling, 88, 89
Sportsman's Dictionary, The, 41
Squires, 10, 12, 19-21 *passim*, 57, 60, 93; guest, 60
Standing the shot, 109
Statues, 29
Stevenage, 94-7
Sticks, 158, 174
Stoats, 16
'Stonehenge', *British Rural Sports*, 12-20, 58-9
Suffolk, 132, 169, 172
Sulphur, burning, 67
Sunday poaching, 19, 20, 41, 96; morning, 10, 28, 58; shooting, 21
Sutherland, 74
Sutton Bridge, 35, 85, 117
Swaledale, 53-5
Swan, 20
Swindgels, 174

Teal, 20, 111

Teesdale, 65, 103
Thorns, 31
Thorpe, Mackenzie, 7, 8, 35, 85, 117
Threshing, 98-9, 119, 122
Tinder box, 80
Todd, Thomas, 65-6, 103
Townsend, Dick, 61-4, 71-3, 75-6, 98-9, 104-6, 110-12, 168-9
Transportation, 19, 43, 140, 165, 175
Trespassing, 14, 20, 35; 'mob-handed', 20
Trevelyan, G.M., *English Social History*, 43
Traps, 103, 111, 138, 140
Tricks, 57-70
Trout, 133
Turkeys, 108
Turnips, 13, 14, 31
Turnpike drains, 103

Violence, 50-2, 140, 143-75

Wagtails, penny, 111
Warwickshire, 10
Watchers/watching, 12, 14, 16, 18, 47, 59, 65-6, 76, 78, 79, 158, 161, 164
Waterfowl, 30

Water rail, 111
Waterton, Charles, 135
Watson, John, 22, 67-9
Wheelwright, Horace William, 'Old Bushman', *Sporting Sketches at Home and Abroad*, 154-63
Whistle, railway, 12, 14
Widgeon, 20, 111
Wife, poacher's, 78, 86, 132
Willock, Colin, *Kenzie the Wild Goose Man*, 35, 117
Willum, Farmer, 25-7
Wiltshire, 174-5
Wine, 30
Wires, 15, 16; heating, 67; trip, 36-8
Women, 71-2, 78, 80, 134-5
Woodcock, 20, 26-7, 60, 111
World War II, 84-5, 104-6
Wrexham, 50-2
Wyman, Harold, *The Great Game*, 36-8, 50-2, 131

Yorkshire, 33-4, 48-9, 53-5, 137

040-677-1